6.45

☞ **W9-BUI-083**

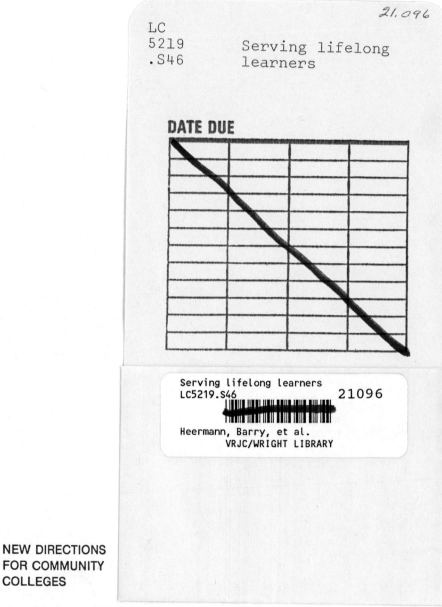
**NEW DIRECTIONS
FOR COMMUNITY
COLLEGES**

Number 29 • 1980

NEW DIRECTIONS FOR COMMUNITY COLLEGES

A Quarterly Sourcebook
Arthur M. Cohen, Editor-in-Chief
Florence B. Brawer, Associate Editor
Sponsored by the ERIC Clearinghouse for Junior Colleges

Number 29, 1980

Serving Lifelong Learners

Barry Heermann
Cheryl Coppeck Enders
Elizabeth Wine
Guest Editors

Jossey-Bass Inc., Publishers
San Francisco • Washington • London

EDUCATIONAL RESOURCES INFORMATION CENTER

ERIC Clearinghouse For Junior Colleges

UNIVERSITY OF CALIFORNIA, LOS ANGELES

SERVING LIFELONG LEARNERS
New Directions for Community Colleges
Volume VIII, Number 1, 1980
Barry Heermann, Cheryl Coppeck Enders, Elizabeth Wine, Guest Editors

New Directions for Community Colleges (publication number 0195-2269)
is published quarterly by Jossey-Bass Inc., Publishers, in association
with the ERIC Clearinghouse for Junior Colleges. Subscriptions are
available at the regular rate for institutions, libraries, and agencies
of $30 for one year. Individuals may subscribe at the special
professional rate of $18 for one year. *New Directions* is numbered
sequentially — please order extra copies by sequential number.
The volume and issue numbers above are included for the
convenience of libraries.

The material in this publication was prepared pursuant to a
contract with the National Institute of Education, U.S.
Department of Health, Education, and Welfare. Contractors
undertaking such projects under government sponsorship are
encouraged to express freely their judgment in professional
and technical matters. Prior to publication, the manuscript
was submitted to the Cooperative Assessment of Experiential
Learning for critical review and determination of professional
competence. This publication has met such standards. Points of
view or opinions, however, do not necessarily represent the
official view or opinions of the Cooperative Assessment of
Experiential Learning or the National Institute of Education.

Correspondence:
Subscriptions, single-issue orders, change of address notices,
undelivered copies, and other correspondence should be sent to
New Directions Subscriptions, Jossey-Bass Inc., Publishers,
433 California Street, San Francisco, California 94104.
Editorial correspondence should be sent to the Editor-in-Chief,
Arthur M. Cohen, at the ERIC Clearinghouse for Junior Colleges,
University of California, Los Angeles, California 90024.

Library of Congress Catalogue Card Number LC 79-92019

Cover design by Willi Baum

Manufactured in the United States of America

This publication was prepared with funding from the National Institute of
Education, U.S. Department of Health, Education, and Welfare under
contract no. 400-78-0038. The opinions expressed in the report do not
necessarily reflect the positions or policies of NIE or HEW.

Contents

Editors' Notes

Alan Tough broke the news. Dozens of educational researchers replicated the findings. The eminently believable Opinion Research Corporation of America legitimized it all. Newspapers across the nation and respected educational journals communicated the revelation: America *is* a nation of lifelong learners.

Alan Tough's findings about adult learning (1978) came as a jolt to American educators. The data substantiated the claim, not taken nearly so seriously, by Ivan Illich in *Deschooling Society:* "We have all learned most of what we know outside of school. Pupils do most of their learning without, and often despite, their teachers" (1970).

The familiar cry to communities and legislatures that institutionalized postsecondary education has the only potential for stimulating a nation of life long learners is a misrepresentation. Only individuals acting autonomously of institutions can choose learning as their way to be in the world. The Tough data substantiate that most Americans, regardless of race, sex, or socioeconomic level, have made that choice, and the choice is affirmation of learning as an integral life pursuit.

The findings from Tough's in-depth, random interviews indicate the following learning patterns for a twelve-month period:

- 90 percent of all adults conduct at least one major learning activity a year
- The average learner conducts five distinct learning projects a year
- The average amount of time spent per learning project is 100 hours (—the average learner spends 500 hours per year engaged in learning projects)
- 73 percent of all learning projects are self-guided
- Only 17 percent of the learning is professionally guided (by proprietary schools, colleges, or company in-service programs)

Tough concludes that in this country there is a pervasive learning myth or stereotype which suggests that most learning is classroom based and institutionally supervised.

The implications of those data for community colleges are especially significant. We have long harbored the notion that the adult populations we serve are somehow not very "together": that they are not self-directed, that they need considerable external control, and that they need structure in order to succeed at learning and growing. The facts are that blue collar and lower middle income families are learning at a rate similar to that of other socioeconomic levels. The content of their learning may be different, but learning— self-directed, independent learning—is something quite integral to life in this age.

The locations for learning are radically different from those previously assumed. The circumstances are different. The methodology is different. The curriculum is different. The "students" are different. Most learning is simply not under our auspices. The curricula of the work place, the home, the family, and the church occupy considerably more of their time than the curriculum of the college.

The implications for community colleges? Before introducing the authors and their lifelong learning responses, we would like to offer some implications of our own:

- We need to aggressively put in place mechanisms for assessing the self-directed learning projects that lifelong learners have initiated prior to entry into our programs
- We need to affirm adults as learners, recognizing their competence, regardless of its source, with academic credit which appropriately relates to our degrees
- We need to be open to the curriculum of the person, adapting flexibly, relying much less on excessively rigid curricula
- We need to be far less concerned with new programs and new courses and more concerned with new ways to learn
- We need to be less preoccupied with control and much more concerned with supporting and guiding students in learning pursuits
- We need to implement learning contract and other nonclassroom, individualized learning strategies for linking students to community resources, beyond the walls of our campus, reinforcing their sense of self-direction and power as lifelong learners

What follows is a smorgasbord of responses to lifelong learning issues. The authors represent a spectrum of on-line practitioners, from an AACJC staff person to a president to a faculty person to a dean, all directly involved in purveying or advocating nontraditional education alternatives for lifelong learners. The colleges represented are the cream of the crop in experimental and lifelong learning: Community College of Vermont, Sinclair Community College, LaGuardia Community College, Whatcom Community College, and Inver Hills Community College.

Who is the lifelong learner? Sheila Gordon grapples with the question in the first chapter, analyzing the demographics, motivation, and environment of the lifelong learner. She offers potential responses that community college educators might provide to their needs.

Peter Smith examines alternative perceptions in light of the learning needs of returning adult students. Chapter Two moves us from a preoccupation with learner to that of faculty, and our author responds to a pivotal concern in the lifelong learning movement: "The New Professional: Professor or Facilitator?"

Program considerations are addressed by Gordon Cowperthwaite in a later chapter. He is critical of that kind of education characterized by the pitcher and mug metaphor: faculty dispense education to passive groups of students as one would pour or top up mugs with a favorite beverage. Cowperthwaite argues for alternatives and new flexibility for lifelong learners that external degree programs afford.

While Cowperthwaite mandates new educational formulas to nurture proactive, lifelong learning, the reality of most community college education is that its lockstep mentality limits that possibility. Learners are conceived as reactive, passive participants in a process centered on information dissemination, housed in facilities representing considerable capital expenditure. How to change the mind-set? Joanne Pertz points the way to those of us anxious to forge new options for learners: a carefully conceived change strategy. She adds, "Of what value is a beautiful dream if it does not become a reality?"

Change agents will need to give attention to attitudes, knowledge, and skills (deliberately in that order) of all of its constituency but particularly its faculty. Frank Christensen addresses the needs of faculty and examines strategies for heightening their competence as lifelong learning facilitators.

Richard Eisele focuses on the counselor role in lifelong learning. Increasingly we have come to understand the false dichotomy of conceiving academic and student activities as separate, autonomous events. Organizationally most community colleges divide their human resources into student and academic service components, cementing the dichotomous relationships. The kind of learning in the realm of personal awareness, value clarification, interpersonal effectiveness, goal setting, and a whole host of affective areas is artificially separated from the more cognitive learning of the traditional academic program. Institutions reflect their own values as credit is awarded for certain kinds of learning and not for others. Eisele offers a model that focuses on the developmental needs of lifelong learners, integrating the services of the institution to that end.

The term *competency based education* has been bandied around for the last ten years. The very nomenclature "competency based" is emotion-charged, causing some educators to recall experiences of pain, tension, and nausea while others are moved to euphoria and ecstasy by its very mention. What precisely is it? What are its implications for lifelong learners? Sharon Hayenga takes on the task.

Linda Reisser discusses mechanisms for recruiting lifelong learners to the kinds of enriched learning environments to which the authors of this *New Directions in Community Colleges* sourcebook allude. Jamison Gilder, in a concluding chapter, causes us to look at the "big picture" as she examines the critical policy questions from her national vantage point with the Lifelong Education component of the American Association of Community and Junior Colleges. In the final chapter Jack Friedlander cites the lifelong learning literature of interest to two-year college educators.

Barry Heermann
Cheryl Coppeck Enders
Elizabeth Wine
Guest Editors

References

Illich, I. D. *Deschooling Society.* New York: Harper & Row, 1971.
Tough, A. "Major Learning Efforts: Recent Research and Future Directions." In K. P. Cross and others (Eds.), *The Adult Learner: Current Issues in Higher Education, 1978.* Washington, D.C.: American Association for Higher Education, 1978.

Barry Heermann has served as a dean and director for Experience Based Education at Sinclair Community College, which includes College Without Walls, Credit for Lifelong Learning, and Field Education programs. He is coordinator of the Council for the Advancement of Experiential Learning's "Community College Network," and is a CAEL Regional Manager for the East Central States.

Cheryl Coppock Enders serves as portfolio faculty person in Sinclair Community College's Credit for Lifelong Learning Program.

SPECIAL NOTE

At Sinclair Community College we have broken new ground, serving lifelong learners in the new way. Elizabeth Wine, post-facilitator and co-editor of this New Directions *sourcebook, has been important to this metamorphosis. Elizabeth died before this sourcebook went to press. We will all miss her greatly. This volume is dedicated to her memory.*

The "lifelong learner" is a category of students full of contradictions, strengths, and weaknesses, bringing challenges and opportunities to community colleges.

Who Is the Lifelong Learner?

Sheila Gordon
Augusta Souza Kappner

The idea of "lifelong learning" in "community" colleges is not new. In one form or another, some kind of continuing education for the lifelong learner has been around for a long time. In an organized form, it has certainly been an American phenomenon since the land grant colleges (spawned through the 1861 Morrill Act) began offering extension courses in agriculture to farmers. In the last half of the nineteenth century there were no community colleges as we now know them; but the land grant institutions provided courses locally where people lived and, in many cases, functioned as sources of secondary education (high schools were not uniformly established until the twentieth century) to countless Americans.

Today's highly complex society demands at least some postsecondary education; the rapidity of change, in turn, requires continuing, or lifelong learning. The community college of today, serving a wide range of students of all ages and backgrounds, both on-campus and off-campus, is thus a central vehicle for perpetuating an established tradition.

The Transformed Educational Context

Although the precedents for lifelong learning opportunities offered in the community are well established, what is happening today is qualitatively different. This difference is manifest in at least four respects. First, the knowledge explosion has created a demand for people to know more and more—and to continually upgrade their knowledge. And, since the knowledge spectrum has expanded so much, the gap between those with a minimal level of education and advanced learning has widened dramatically.

Secondly, the knowledge explosion has been accompanied by growth of organized—and competitive—learning options: open access community colleges; YMCA's, museums, churches, and similar agencies; in-house industry-run training; individualized instruction and contract learning; computerized learning; distance learning through television "colleges"; and the omnipresence of television, itself. The options and invitations to learn are everywhere, besieging people through bus and subway ads, in newspapers and magazines, on radio and television, in the workplace. Register by mail, charge it through Master Charge, take courses at the office, study by correspondence—the persistent message is come back to learn.

Third, the notion of the adult has changed to accomodate the idea of lifelong learning. Until recently, the popular conception—even the scientific view—of adulthood was that once one "matured" one was an adult and there was little further development. Erikson's (1968), Levinson's (1978) and others' work in adult stages of development has changed that; and Gail Sheehy's best selling *Passages* (1976) has made commonplace the idea of different stages of growth after twenty-one! Since growth and change now seem an inevitability, continued education is even more attractive to adults.

Fourth, there is heightened emphasis on lifelong learning. In fact, it even has its own new and accepted name—*lifelong learning*—an alliterative, if ambiguous term which has had currency for no more than four years. Whether ongoing learning has become fashionable because of the various social and intellectual forces or whether the demographic pressures on higher education have forced institutions to cater to adults is an insoluble question. The fact is that attention to the adult learner has become a focus of public policy and the concern of many institutions.

Who Is the Lifelong Learner Today?

Expanding Numbers. The number and proportion of students over twenty-two in higher education is expanding. This reflects both increased participation on the part of adults and the changing demographic patterns in which our general population is "aging." By the year 2000, persons between the ages of thirty and fifty will be the majority of the population (Golladay, 1976). A study of institutions reporting extensive change in their recruitment emphasis shows a dramatic increase in attention to adults (Shulman, 1976)—from 38 percent of institutions to 66 percent. Another study conducted by the National Center for Education Statistics (Oakes, 1976) shows that participation in adult education increased three times as much as the eligible population. Today more than half the community college enrollment nationwide is part-time. The authors' observations of their own and other community colleges reveal a pattern where the average age of community college students is well up in the twenties—if not older.

Why the Return to School? In addition to the educational forces triggered by the knowledge explosion, a number of social forces have been at work which are spurring adults to become more active lifelong learners.

Some of these forces emerged from the ferment of the 1960s and the emphasis on activism, especially for groups previously excluded. Thus minority groups and women (returning to work as well as upgrading) especially, form important subsets of the adults who are advancing themselves and moving into the mainstream via higher education. Moreover, Vietnam veterans armed with G.I. Bill benefits and poor employment prospects have also filled the ranks of adult students. The overall economic contraction, coupled with the press of inflation, has led many to pursue higher education as a way to maximize their job flexibility and income picture. Still another group is emerging as important: the preretirement age group and senior citizens who are growing in numbers and seek leisure pursuits and intellectual stimulation. Finally, a large and growing number of adults are seeking to remedy basic education deficiencies in language and mathematics. This group includes numerous persons for whom English is not their dominant language (Hispanic and Indo-Chinese, for example).

What we find overall is a complex of reasons motivating adults to continued education—self-fulfillment; career change or upgrading, including return to work; basic education; and leisure pursuits. Moreover, we find that many students combine two or more reasons.

Characteristics and Contradictions. The adults we see returning to school are—individually and collectively—full of contradictions, strengths, and weaknesses.

They are, first of all, *experienced*. Compared to the conventional eighteen-year-old student they bring with them rich backgrounds. They have served in the army; they have traveled; they have raised families and coped with the various stages of childhood, teenage problems, divorce, illness, and deaths; they have balanced budgets—or creditors; they have seen neighborhoods change; they have worked in all kinds of settings, under all kinds of pressures. And though they tend to lack the intellectual framework, they have learned a great deal experientially—often more than their college instructors—about psychology, or economics, or politics.

Not only have our prospective adult students learned from experience, they are also active, organized learners. Allen Tough of the Ontario Institute of Studies in Education estimates that some 79–98 percent of adults are lifelong learners, whom he defines as people who engage in a learning project, "a highly deliberate effort to gain and retain a defined area of knowledge or a skill, or to change in some other way . . . (with activities) totalling at least seven hours" (1979, p. 9). Tough's ingenious study of a wide range of adults showed that 80–90 percent of the adult population conducts at least one learning project each year, and the typical adult conducts five distinct learning projects per year, spending 100 hours on each project. In addition, Tough and researchers who have followed his lead have found that only 20 percent of all learning projects are planned by a professional (for instance, a teacher), whereas 80 percent are self-planned (Tough, 1979); and in self-planned learning, the learner manages his or her own learning and incorporates some sustained help from over ten other persons (Tough, 1967). The learning is thus quite different from that offered in colleges, where, in contrast, the emphasis is on teacher-directed instruction where, moreover, students are not expected to seek help from others or to learn collaboratively.

While the lifelong learner does bring experience and self-directed learning skills, he or she also brings some problems. First, the rich experiences derive from what is typically a complex life — which persists while the person is in school. A child may get sick, economic pressures may impinge, shopping must get done and meals made, crises erupt. The result may often be erratic attendance patterns, certainly not the regularized sequential semester patterns our catalogues suggest. Moreover, the need to request "incompletes" is typically well justified. Money and time are cited by adults as the greatest obstacles to learning.

In addition to these real life pressures, many adults — particularly those who would come to community colleges — are also saddled with serious basic skills deficiencies. The Adult Functional Competency Study (Northcutt, 1975, pp. 6–8) reveals the stunning fact that some one fifth of U.S. adults are "functioning with difficulty" in the areas of writing, computation, problem solving, reading, community resources, health, government and law, consumer economics, and occupational knowledge. Even 20 percent of those who have completed high school or college fail within these categories. And, predictably, in contrast to the population at large, these adults are poorer and lower skilled, more likely to be unemployed, and to be Black or Hispanic. These are the populations community colleges — with their open access mission — are expected to serve.

Program Implications. Clearly, the lifelong learner has a set of characteristics which require institutional responses unlike those normally associated with most colleges. In particular, adults have strong preferences for flexibility, convenience and individualization (Penland, 1977). And, as Tough (1978, p. 9) suggests, to serve adults colleges need to shift their emphasis from "providing education or instruction . . . (to) facilitating relevant learning."

To adapt effectively to adults, we need to consider all the components of our operations: admissions, scheduling and administrative procedures, counseling, crediting and delivery academic learning, and faculty.

Admissions. Colleges that conduct individualized admissions screening will have to begin to include criteria such as motivation, career performance, and previous experience. For older applicants the years between their last formal education and admission to the new program may carry more weight than past academic performance. Similarly, admissions requirements should not involve review of high school records in a manner not applicable to the adult who completed high school many years ago. Lack of information and rusty test-taking skills often make placement or admissions examinations more anxiety provoking for an adult than for the recent high school graduate. Unnecessary testing should be avoided and mechanisms developed for identifying and separating test-taking skills from subject mastery.

Administrative Procedures. Registration and orientation processes at most college campuses are at best frustrating and inconvenient to the adult participant. Location and timing of such processes are generally geared to capturing the largely available day population. Administrative offices are often not open evenings and weekends. Quite often time-consuming lines are involved. Forms often require information which, though historically and habitually collected in universities, may not be relevant for an adult learner. On the other hand, assumptions are often made as to the general familiarity of students with academic administrative procedures which may have changed over the ten to twenty years that an adult may have been away from school. Many institutions have time limits for degree completion that, although appropriate for the full-time younger student, may be detrimental to the adult student. Given the prevalence of the need to "stop out" among adults, definitions of attrition and drop out must be revised and nonpunitive procedures for stopping out and returning must be implemented.

Counseling and Financial Aid. Academic advisement, personal counseling, and financial aid advisement are often scarce for students not in a conventional day pattern. Although half of the community college enrollment nationwide is part-time, tuition aid programs are generally not available for part-time students. Self-supporting adults with dependents often find tuition a barrier to college attendance. Colleges may also be prepared to devote some of their own resources to financial aid for part-time students. Nationwide many continuing education programs are designed to be self-supporting, thus forcing the adult, regardless of income, to pay fees for which no financial aid is available. Even where corporate financed education is a possibility, it is often targeted to middle level management.

Crediting and Delivering Academic Learning. If colleges accept adults as active learners with a substantial learning history, then creative ways of integrating formal and informal, past and present learning will emerge. Colleges will need to have several enrollment options to adequately meet the interests of the adult learner: credit, noncredit, audit, and so on. Movement from noncredit to credit and vice versa should be administratively facilitated. Colleges which don't already do so should consider the recognition and acceptance of credit by examination mechanisms such as CLEP and the less traditional individualized assessment techniques such as portfolio development.

Relatedly, colleges need to consider expanding the independent study/contract learning options available to adult and evening students.

Faculty. Receptivity of faculty to the changes required in serving adults varies with the institutions and with the individual faculty member. Every campus has its "core" of faculty who are obviously dedicated to the needs of the adult learner. Other faculty are resistant to changes which affect their teaching schedules and methodology.

At LaGuardia Community College we are currently experiencing the first experimental year of an Alternative Degree Program which was designed to introduce a contract learning model within the institution. Over the past months it has become very apparent to us that the role transition from "teacher" to "mentor" is one fraught with difficulty. It is a transition which, even when involving the most skilled and highly motivated classroom instructors, requires orientation, assistance, and consistent organizational support.

An institution experiencing a shift to adult learners should review its criteria for teachers and administrators and seek to attract individuals capable of integrating subject matter with life and work experiences, willing to abdicate the "only authority" role, and willing to fulfill the advisement and counseling roles necessary for working with adult learners. Counselors similarly will need to accept a greater responsibility for assisting with learning resources and building support systems for students that extend beyond their institution. Most educational institutions do not enjoy the luxury of new personnel recruitment in these financially pressed times. This fact makes the need for professional development of counselors, faculty members, and administrators a high priority.

In addition to modifying our own programs in these several ways, accomodating adults may lead community colleges into new collaborative efforts. We can join together with a wide range of other institutions to offer information, counseling, and referral services to meet the need which the high school guidance counselor and peers may provide for the eighteen-year-old. We can join with other community organizations to conduct local assessments of unmet lifelong educational needs. We also need to be prepared to join the legislative efforts to increase financial aid to part-time students.

Adapting our inevitably bureaucratic institutions to adults is not easy, nor inexpensive. But the cost benefits are demonstrable: an exciting and large pool of students, bringing new perspectives and strengthened enrollments to our institutions.

Conclusion

If any college can serve the lifelong learner, it is the community college. In contrast to four-year colleges and universities, the community college's orientation has been toward serving a wide range of students and toward using unconventional off-campus locations. On the other hand, as this chapter's attention to program implications suggests, there are counter-balancing factors within the institutions (such as lack of services in the evening, resistance to crediting prior learning, curricula—especially remedial programs—ill-adapted to adults).

It is the bias of the authors that community colleges should make concerted efforts to serve lifelong learners, particularly the less advantaged adults. It seems likely, moreover, that such a mission for community colleges will become even more important in the future than it has been. We tend to share K. Patricia Cross's suggestion that "it is quite possible that adult and continuing education could replace college degrees as the socioeconomic sorter of American society. Employers, instead of asking about college degrees, may begin to ask potential employees what they have done the past few years to keep abreast of the rapidly changing world" (1978, p. 4). What, then, would happen to presently poorly educated adults, who are disproportionately minority, women, and the aged? They would suffer a kind of double jeopardy, being then twice removed from the tools needed for competition in the job market. It is here, in our opinion, that the community college can play a major role and fulfill an important social responsibility by ensuring access for these individuals to a wide range of degree and nondegree options.

Community colleges must resist the temptation to compete solely for the lucrative leisure time needs of lifelong learners and must instead fulfill a genuine social responsibility to lessen the gap between adults with formal education and those without. The "If It's Tuesday, It Must Be T'ai Chi" population (Kantrowitz, 1979) has many opportunities and options from which to choose. The adult without a high school diploma or with a recent GED has needs which can be best served in a community college. Community colleges must work against the predictors of participation in education to meet these needs.

References

Cross, K. P. "The Adult Learner." In K. P. Cross and others (Eds.), *The Adult Learner. Current Issues in Higher Education, 1978.* Washington, D.C.: American Association for Higher Education, 1978.

Erikson, E. H. *Identity: Youth and Crisis.* New York: Norton, 1968.

Golladay, M. A. *The Condition of Education. A Statistical Report on the Condition of Education in the United States.* Washington, D.C.: National Center for Education Statistics. U.S. Government Printing Office, 1976.

Kantrowitz, B. "If It's Tuesday, It Must Be T'ai Chi." *The New York Times,* January 7, 1979, Section 13, p. 1.

Levinson, D. J. *The Seasons of a Man's Life.* New York: Random House, 1978.

Northcutt, N. and others. *Adult Functional Competency: A Summary.* Austin: Division of Extension, Industrial and Business Training Bureau, University of Texas, 1975.

Oakes, I. E. *Participation in Adult Education: May 1972.* Washington, D.C.: National Center for Education Statistics, 1976.

Penland, P. R. *Individual Self-Planned Learning in America.* Final report of project 475AH60058 under grant no. G007603327, U.S. Office of Education, Office of

Libraries and Learning Resources. Pittsburgh: Graduate School of Library and Information Sciences, University of Pittsburgh, 1977.

Sheehy, G. *Passages: Predictable Crises of Adult Life.* New York: Dutton, 1976.

Shulman, C. H. *Enrollment Trends in Higher Education.* ERIC/Higher Education Research Report No. 6. Washington, D.C.: ERIC Clearinghouse on Higher Education and American Association for Higher Education, 1976.

Tough, A. *Learning Without a Teacher: Tasks and Assistance During Self-Planned Learning Projects.* Toronto: Ontario Institute for Studies in Education, 1967.

Tough, A. "Major Learning Efforts: Recent Research and Future Directions." In K. P. Cross and others (Eds.), *The Adult Learner. Current Issues in Higher Education, 1978.* Washington, D.C.: American Association for Higher Education, 1978.

Sheila Gordon is associate dean of cooperative education at LaGuardia Community College. She also serves as vice chairperson of CAEL (Council for the Advancement of Experiential Learning).

Augusta Souza Kappner is dean of continuing education at LaGuardia Community College. She also serves as chairperson of the City University Council of Community College Deans of Continuing Education, Evening and Summer Sessions.

The lifelong learning movement — new kinds of learning, new learners in new places — demands a reassessment of the traditional definition of the educational profession.

The New Professional: Professor or Facilitator?

Peter P. Smith

Educators have long debated the question of whether or not education is indeed a profession. The question has yet to be fully resolved. However, the emergence of the lifelong learning movement puts the traditional definitions and structures of higher education to the test. At the heart of the matter is the question of whether the traditional roles of the classroom teacher and the campus will change in response to an emerging generation of learners and learning needs which are neither sequential, predictable, nor orderly in the manner to which educators have become accustomed.

Lifelong learning and its companion, experiential learning, are far more than passing fads. They are symptoms of the age of information — an age when people work continuously to stay current with the world as it develops and changes around them. Historically, parents could assume that the skills necessary for their children to make their way in the world were similar to the skills which they and their fathers and mothers had had. No more. Now parents must work on their own growth, knowing that personal as well as technical demands will continue to change in an age of accelerating information growth.

By the same token, lifelong learning is more than a handy slogan developed by public relations agencies to explain the broad array of educational alternatives that have cropped up over the last decade. It is a phrase that symbolizes an emerging focus on the learner and learning; and a move away from the teacher and teaching in postsecondary education. It says that we spend a great deal of time throughout our lives educating ourselves. I am not suggesting that structured higher education is insignificant. But I *am* saying that the importance of that part of our total educational experience is overstated.

Lifelong learning raises a host of difficult, ticklish, and profound questions for education and educators. The questions challenge conventional thinking about curriculum, learning sites, evaluation, and student achievement, not to mention teaching. We must ask what it means to be educated for the twenty-first century, and we must ask what professional tools are necessary to accomplish that job. If we think that repackaging Plato, offering old wine in new bottles and at new tables, will satisfy the appetite for lifelong learning, I believe we are wrong.

Being Educated for the Twenty-first Century

We are in an era of information, leaving behind the time when the very scarcity of information and organized knowledge necessitated pooling it for more efficient and effective dissemination. Traditionally, professors grouped themselves in enclaves to better pool their resources and students went to them as readily and as similarly as Americans currently go to the gas station.

Lifelong and experiential education challenge the traditional assumptions of the academy. As the patterns of information management and learner participation have changed, pressure has increased for institutions to change the ways in which they relate to learners and to information, both structurally and functionally.

Learners in the information-rich twenty-first century are going to need to know how to process and reference information, how to make the welter of information and knowledge work for them. It will become the mark of an educated person that they know how they learn, know what they want to learn, and where and how much.

Teaching versus Facilitating

If we accept the world and life as our teacher, what is the specific origin, nature, and purpose of a college program or faculty? The answer lies in a reinterpretation of the education profession around qualities in the teaching-learning cycle that transcend the setting, the curriculum, or the academic level.

We might well ask ourselves: How is college teaching similar to other educational levels and settings — vocational, technical, elementary, early childhood, secondary? There are commonalities, but little work has been done to bind the common elements of the teaching profession together, regardless of level or setting. In fact, most educators focus on the learning setting and the curriculum to highlight the *differences* among educational endeavors. The life-long learning movement underscores this lack by requiring a focus on professional abilities instead of on setting or curriculum per se.

The philosophical base of education has been explicated for years, by Dewey, Whitehead, and a host of others; and a variety of approaches has been with us almost as long in the form of such institutions as Antioch and Goddard which look at learning instead of curriculum as their primary focus. These colleges blended work and other experiences into the learning mix because they believed that a mixture of theory and practice would lead to a stronger educational program. Happily, the evolution of our information-rich society makes the question of a clear professional base more than simply academic. More people are seeking learning throughout life and fewer people are seeking education in the traditional manner. We need professional tools and definitions to go with the philosophy and examples we have and the reality we face.

The answer lies in a shift of focus from setting and curriculum to four areas of expertise that are generic to the learning process and essential tools for the professional who wants to help. Every learning situation, regardless of level or setting, should be analyzed from the points of view of assessment, planning, implementation, and evaluation. All teachers are concerned with these questions when they are doing their job:

1. Assess: Diagnosing student skills, abilities, and readiness for the curriculum or learning situation in question.
2. Plan: Organizing material, situations, and other resources to maximize the possibility of successful teaching and learning.
3. Implement: Teaching, experiencing, studying, and feeling the learning through the subject matter being shared.
4. Evaluate: Ascertaining how the learner has changed as a result of the educational effort that has taken place, and documenting that change.

Most educators perform some variation of these functions as they organize learning experiences for their students. For instance, a professor of Shakespeare will not offer graduate level work to college freshmen, nor will a chemistry professor confuse organic chemistry with an introductory course. The educational profession should look for its identity in a set of activities and related abilities that allow the individual to move beyond level and subject matter as indicators of either quality or professional identity. Professional educators should be able to assess, plan, implement, and evaluate learning with the twin goals of sharing knowledge and teaching the learning skills to their students.

If we accept the premise that information processing skills are going to be a mark of educated persons in the future, then an integral part of their education should be focused on helping them learn how to diagnose their own situation, organize information, learn, and know what and how much they have learned. As professional educators, we want our students to learn these information processing skills so that they may become conscious lifelong learners. For the professional, it means shifting the major focus from that of teacher to that of facilitator of learning.

Discussion

There are reasons beyond the moral imperative why these functions should be considered. The change in student behaviors is already upon us — fewer students exist, more people are learning in alternative settings, irreverence for a "college education" is growing, political skepticism abounds, and financial costs are escalating daily. Moreover, research shows that learning goes on throughout life on a regular and organized basis that, for the most part, has nothing to do with postsecondary education.

It is not simply happenstance that learner behavior, economic and demographic forces, and research findings all point in the same direction. They are all responding to the same general forces in society. The emerging role of the educator must respond also by becoming that of diagnostician, processor of knowledge and information, and evaluator.

In this context the traditional teaching role continues to be one of several ways that the implementing function can be accomplished. However, the person who can "only" teach will have the status of a technician in relationship to the profession as a whole. The emerging multifaceted role of the educator is that of a facilitator who, beyond teaching students new and needed content (facts, skills) teaches them how to learn.

The true potential in the lifelong learning and experiential education movements is for educators as well as learners. The new settings and kinds of learning call for an updated structure for the profession. The functions of assessment, planning, implementation, and evaluation form a base for the consideration of all planned educational programs, on the one hand, and all learning that can be documented on the other. For the lifelong learner, they mean an opportunity to look at and be assisted in learning ventures which respond to articulated learning needs. They provide an avenue to better quality control, better service, and a broader professional context.

Peter P. Smith was the founder and first president of the Community College of Vermont.

Gaining institutional acceptance and continuing support for lifelong learning programs in higher education is certainly essential and frequently difficult. The time to develop strategies for programs' institutionalization is at their inception; this will help to avoid mistakes and oversights that may hinder the programs' adoption by their institutions.

The ABC's of Institutionalizing Lifelong Learning Programs

Joanne L. Pertz

Of what value is a beautiful dream if it does not become a reality? Of what use are well-designed lifelong learning projects if they do not become permanent programs? How many creative pilot projects have "died on the vine" because they were not integrated as ongoing components of their institutions? This waste of resources—human and financial—is particularly lamentable during these days of shrinking higher education dollars, and the loss of lifelong learning options is regrettable during this era of increasing numbers of nontraditional students.

What characterizes institutionalization of a program on a campus? By definition, it puts the program "in the care of" the institution. This includes official approval by appropriate parties, such as curriculum committees, faculty governance groups, administrative councils, deans, and chancellors. The program is officially recognized on campus, as well as by other postsecondary institutions, accrediting bodies, and related groups, and is readily accessible to the students for whom it was designed. A prime indicator of institutionalization is the tangible evidence: the institution's commitment to the program through appropriations of budget monies and assignment of faculty, staff, space, and equipment.

What can we, as developers and advocates of lifelong learning programs, do to gain their acceptance and adoption by our institutions? Let us examine some ABC's—Aids, Barriers, and Cautions—involved in institution-alizing lifelong learning programs.

Aids

Goals and Needs. To begin with, our programs should be based on sound academic theories and principles. They should be congruent with our institutions' missions, goals, and resources and not duplicate or compete with existing programs and services. The program designs should grow out of established and documented needs of the students and potential students in the communities served; they should not be "canned" programs from other campuses adopted in toto but should be adaptations responding to the uniqueness of each situation.

Declining Enrollments. Current status of student enrollment trends in higher education is one of our greatest allies in gaining acceptance for life-long options. Cross and Florio (1978, p. 18) point out that "colleges and universities, short of money and prompted by declining enrollments among the traditional college-age population, are actively reorienting themselves to put forth the effort to seek out and serve the needs of other types of students." Eurich concurs, stating (Cross and Florio, 1978, p. viii) that "college and university administrators are beginning to realize that the expanding pool of older people represents a significant source of new students . . . (and) are beginning to develop special programs for older people." Lifelong learning programs cater to this sizable potential clientele.

Involvement. There should be a broad base of involvement in planning, implementing, and evaluating the programs with democratic provision for input into these developmental phases by all parties affected by them, as well as others likely to react publicly to them. When the programs involve businesses, agencies, and other noncollegiate institutions, their personnel should be included in the planning; their needs integrated into the program designing; and their active support secured in the initial stages through corroborative letters to funding agencies, regents, legislators, and faculty groups or by pledges of training funds from their often sizable education budgets. Public attention should be drawn to the positive contribution these programs will make to the upgrading of employees' training; the revitalization of the college faculty, enabling them to better serve these "new" students; and the attraction of a different group of students to enrich the student body makeup and swell the enrollment figures. Other benefits to the community at large, unique to each project, should be effectively pointed out through well-chosen media channels.

Communication. Open, honest sharing of the programs' progress with appropriate publics should be planned carefully; these may include faculty, students, other potential consumers, governing bodies, legislators, funding sources, and others. These progress reports, however, should be controlled by the program staff since concepts and facts, as well as accomplishments and inadequacies, can be presented in varying ways, some of which may unnecessarily shed a negative light on the program. For example, information presented incompletely or out of context may be misleading and official enrollment figures may not reflect the total number benefitting from the programs. Budgeting for professional consultation in this area may be money well spent (as profit-making organizations learned long ago); the right logo or brochure may make a decided difference in the reception the program receives from its various audiences.

Evaluation. In these days of increased demand for accountability, program evaluation should be built from the beginning of the project. The evaluation process should be feasible and produce adequate hard data on a continuing basis as efficiently as possible. It should be an "all purpose" system that will provide the various types and quantity of data required in the future without unnecessary information that will result in waste of time and money.

Realities. To gain permanence, programs must be planned around political and economic realities—not only today's, which are hard enough to grasp, but tomorrow's, under which the programs will continue to function. These are certainly too complex and unique to discuss at length here; suffice it to say that intimate, continuing contacts with legislative, faculty governance, and funding groups are crucial to deal with these challenges adequately.

Personnel. The people involved in planning and implementing a lifelong learning program can hold the key to its success or failure. Those chosen to be an integral part of it should be well respected (to some observers this means having "faculty credentials"); fully qualified to handle the demanding and assorted responsibilities; and supportive of the basic philosophy and concepts of lifelong learning as well as those of the specific program in question. Gradually the personnel base should be widened to include "voluntary converts" to serve as advisory board members, liaison, PR representatives, and so on. All of those who participate in the program—faculty, academic staff, clerical staff, and professionals from the community—should be rewarded as generously as is feasible, not only monetarily (when possible) but also with written and oral acknowledgment or appreciation, tenure file or employer letters, campus recognition, merit awards, and released time. Hiring personnel already employed at the campus often is advantageous if they are well qualified, particularly in these days of "tenured-in" faculty. Some situations may dictate against this; a highly qualified and recognized professional with no prior association with the campus may give the program more status and needed neutrality. The issue must be studied at length for the best hiring decision in each particular project.

Barriers

Finances. There are a number of obstacles that can impede a program's progress toward becoming institutionalized. Perhaps the most obvious barriers are financial problems which can take many forms and shapes.

There can be inadequate funding due to insufficient appropriations, budget cutbacks, restrictive use of appropriated funds, short-term funding, or requirements for program self-support. When we realize the many public and private agencies and foundations that have monies available for lifelong learning programming, we may then label our funding problem as "lack of skills to successfully obtain appropriate funding" rather than inadequate funding. Many institutions and persons assigned to design lifelong learning programs are not aware of the many sources where they may request monies for the planning and implementing of their programs; they lack grantsmanship expertise or perhaps the initiative to submit proposals requesting funding. Consultants can be hired to perform this task or the skills can be quickly learned by faculty and staff members who can read and follow instructions. The challenge is to discover the most appropriate funding source for your needs and then plan for continuing funding when the initial soft monies will be terminated.

Staffing. Staffing problems which can seriously hamper the success of a program include being understaffed (adequate clerical staff is particularly essential to the success of a new project); having unqualified personnel (short-term contracts and underpaid positions make it difficult to attract and hold well-qualified persons); and lacking clearly defined personnel responsibilities and procedures (doing the wrong job well is a hollow victory).

Space and Equipment. Lack of adequate space in which to function or poor location from which to operate can often be a serious deterrent to a program's success. Sufficient, appropriately located program space should be bargained for early in the planning game. Adequate funds for needed equipment and supplies should be written into the initial budget.

The other side of the coin reveals that excessive staffing, space, and equipment assigned to a project may result in resentment by other professionals and program staffs. Original project funding should be exact enough to avoid this abuse. If, as program directors, we have no control over this and are saddled with an overage of staff or supplies, we can, at least, not flaunt them and judiciously offer to share them with other programs that are more needful or with whom it is important to establish good relationships. (Funding regulations shold be adhered to in this sharing procedure.)

Time Restraints. Too little time to cover all fronts and keep all of the fences mended can be detrimental to acceptance of new programs. Final program acceptance and institutionalization is largely dependent on positive relationships between the program staff and those who make the decisions. These take time to develop! A minimum of two years is probably necessary to develop a program and lay the firm foundation needed for eventual acceptance. Initial budget proposals should be based on realistic time frames, and designs for evaluation should not expect useful hard data in the first six months of program operation. Approval procedures can be very time-consuming, such as waiting for an essential committee to have its quarterly meeting or for a key professor to return from sabbatical in France.

Communication. Negative publicity—or lack of any visibility—can kill a program. Opposition, lack of understanding or support, and apathy by faculty, administration, boards, and students that is openly communicated to others can be deadly.

Resistance. Now a word of warning about the damage that can be caused by covert, as well as overt, resistance. Gaff (1978, p.44) warns that "liberal reformers frequently underestimate or ignore resistance and assume that their ideas will be embraced by others. As a result, they have unrealistic aspirations, expecting changes to be more massive and to appear more quickly than is reasonable and thereby setting themselves and their supporters up for inevitable failure . . . . It is important, therefore, for would-be reformers to recognize resistance and to understand why it exists, in order to identify steps that can be taken to gain the support of those affected by a proposed change."

At the risk of stereotyping, it might be useful to identify several types of personalities that tend to hinder institutionalization of programs: defenders of the status quo, empire builders building competing projects, political enemies, the perennial "anti-" advocates, and budget fanatics. Does your campus harbor any of these?

Rules and Regulations. Internal and external policies and rules, statutory regulations, and cumbersome procedures can impede progress toward program acceptance. These should be carefully scrutinized early in the planning stage to identify those that must be complied with and others where requesting exemptions might be more appropriate. Certainly it is important to follow the usual campus procedures for program approval—routing the program proposal through the required committees, boards, councils, senates, deans, and so on. Attempting to shortcut these "sacred channels" would only hurt the program by creating distrust and suspicion in those who believe in the necessity of this procedure. A program proposal's safe journey through all these passageways should "purify" it so that it is then "above reproach." The correct chain of command should be studied and not deviated from unless there is a very valid reason; the top administrator on a campus is often the best advisor in these matters. Guiding the proposal through the required procedures, plus some additional ones for good measure, is often a very political process; it may involve bargaining for shared use of funds or facilities, designing a "banking" plan to compensate faculty for time they spend on your program, and agreeing to support another program in return for their support for yours. Ambiguous or disputed interpretations of statutory regulations or policies can further complicate this process. Interpretations may need to be requested from appropriate legal authorities, perhaps ending up in the attorney general's office.

In procedural matters, ignorance is no excuse. It is the program staff's responsibility to understand and complete the necessary steps to clear the way for final approval by the institution—and at the system level, if needed. Budget procedures and deadlines are essential for staff to follow. It is advisable to chart out a two-year calendar of activities and deadlines for the project, revising it as needed—which may be continually.

18

Cautions

Danger Signs. In aiming at gaining acceptance for lifelong learning programs, watch out for the following:
- Lowering of academic standards
- Tokenism or lip service only from decision makers—with no action to back it up
- "One person shows" where a program becomes associated with a personality rather than an activity or service
- The impossible and unnecessary task of trying to win over *everyone*
- Administration's ideas imposed from the top downward
- Faculty collective bargaining agreements without provisions for nontraditional faculty and staff scheduling and workload assignments
- Hard sell techniques that grate against our academic orientations; let the programs sell themselves
- Lack of flexibility in implementation that does not allow responsiveness to changing needs and resources
- Pie in the sky objectives that are unrealistic with the time and money provided
- Short-term commitments
- Premature—and other unrealistic—requirements for hard data
- The three "softies"—soft monies, soft data, and soft staff who do not defend the program when they should

A Model

Participatory Project Planning Process. A suggested approach to implementing lifelong learning projects and other nontraditional programs in higher education that helps assure institutional and community acceptance is the Participatory Project Planning Process, used in the FIPSE funded Non-collegiate Institutional Learning Project in the Community College System of the University of Hawaii (Pertz, 1978). The major innovative element of this process is a series of meetings or action sessions of the groups to be affected by the resultant program. In these sessions, homogeneous groupings of concerned parties are informed about the project and provided with an opportunity for input into the planning process. Thus, the project becomes *their* project; they have a stake in the planning of it and, therefore, in the *success* of it. Their critiques and suggestions are voiced during the design stage when they can be integrated creatively. Their ideas are heard, considered on their merits, and handled through incorporation into the design or by discarding with explanations of their inappropriateness. The specific givens for the project are made clear at the beginning of each session so that the parameters are understood and respected. The issues to be considered and decisions to be made in the planning process are arranged in logical sequence, then the appropriate group chosen to consider each issue or decision (for instance, deans of students to deliberate and take action on crediting considerations).

The action groups meet in this sequential order; their decisions build upon those of the preceding groups. As the planning layers are laid one upon another by each succeeding group, the total project design emerges. Where a specific issue is considered by more than one action group and their recommendations are not congruous, the program staff arbitrates, justifying their decision in writing to both groups. This points to an essential characteristic of the process—open communication, achieved through numerous face to face contacts and also by printed materials: information sheets, lists of issues, session reports, and summaries.

This approach might be compared to a football game. The "referees" (project staff) explain the "rules" (guidelines) by which the proposal and system allow the planning "game" to be played. After each "play" (action session) is completed, the referees write a play by play account of the action and the results of the game on the "scoresheet" (action session report) and distribute it to all concerned: "players" (participants in that action session), "former players" (participants in previous action sessions), and "interested spectators" (provosts, deans, faculty, legislators, and other interested parties). Commentary on the play is solicited and considered by the referees who are ultimately held accountable for the outcome of the game and the final decisions. They are cautious to "blow the whistle" (veto decisions and actions) only when necessary since they know the players can, in fact, "walk off the field" (not support and thereby defeat the project). Note that "body contact" (free exchange of ideas) is encouraged, "tackling" (confrontation) is allowed, but "interference" (emotional critiques or trying to change the givens) is illegal. At all times during the play, the focus is kept on the "goal" (serving the students and community). The "press reviews" (public relations) can greatly affect the morale and confidence of the players and spectators and must be handled skillfully and judiciously.

Above all, the referees in such a game must have great faith in the caliber of players and their ability and desire to play the game fairly; they also must believe unswervingly in the goal. It is possible for the referees to be "clobbered" (rejected or have the project sabotaged) by the players if they lose respect for the officials and/or the way the "game is being called" (project is being managed).

Philosophical Basis. This Participatory Project Planning Process is based on the PIP Formula, as follows:

Participation ⟶ Involvement ⟶ Possession

This is to say that when persons participate actively and willingly in a planning process, they will become intellectually, emotionally, and physically involved. This leads to identification with and feeling a part of the process, personally as well as professionally; this represents an investment in the project. Once people invest in something (buy stock in a company), they become a part of it and actually possess a portion of that in which they invest. The project, or company, is partly theirs. Therefore, they try to help it become as successful as it can be, supporting it through their contributions of time, good will, positive public relations, and so on.

A second premise is that most people have suggestions and ideas worth considering, especially regarding projects that have a direct effect on them. A corollary of this is that most persons are reasonable about reaching consensus and not insisting that their way is the only way.

In addition, the process assumes that the project staff, though ultimately accountable for the project's outcome, do not have all the answers; that they can learn from interaction with others interested in the project; and, even though the staff may have conceptualized the project in a particular way, that another model may be more ideal when all the facts, needs, and opinions are considered.

A further assumption is based on a preventive medicine concept — that discovering ailments or problems early in the process makes them easier to treat or respond to than after the project design is complete. When policies and procedures are etched in stone, it is much harder to chisel changes in them than when they have just been sketched in chalk.

Results. Ideally, the skillful use of such a planning process will result in a program that (1) responds to the actual needs as perceived by the parties concerned, (2) makes use of the expertise and experience of many diverse experts, and (3) gains the support and acceptance of the parties concerned early in the planning process. Even though this approach may involve more time, effort, and risk, the resultant program should be a much better candidate for institutional acceptance than one planned by a few people and forced on the many parties that are ultimately going to be affected by the program.

Conclusion

Though the goal of gaining institutional acceptance for our lifelong learning programs may be a difficult one to achieve, it is without a doubt one for which we, as lifelong learning designers and advocates, must plan and strive. By identifying the necessary procedures to be completed and the obstructions that may need to be overcome, we should have a better chance of institutionalizing our programs.

References

Cross, W., and Florio, C. *You Are Never Too Old to Learn*. New York: McGraw-Hill, 1978.

Gaff, J. G. (Ed.). *New Directions for Higher Education: Institutional Renewal Through the Improvement of Teaching*, no. 24. San Francisco: Jossey-Bass, 1978.

Pertz, L. *Final Report.* Noncollegiate Institutional Learning Project (FIPSE-funded). Honolulu: University of Hawaii Community College System, 1978.

Joanne L. Pertz is currently doing advanced study in educational administration, policy, and social planning at Harvard University. From 1976 to 1978 she planned and implemented two innovative programs within the University of Hawaii: the College Credit Equivalency Program at Leeward Community College and the Noncollegiate Institutional Learning Project within the Community College System. She has also been on the staff of the extended degree program at the University of Wisconsin at Green Bay.

Graduate institutions and directors of college in-service activities
must be responsible for preparing faculty to deal with the
ever increasing number of adult learners.

Equipping Faculty to Serve Lifelong Learners

Frank Christensen

Robert Wilson walked into his Thursday evening American history class and suddenly realized that he was the youngest person in the room. Because of declining enrollment in the daytime Data Processing program, Eugene Collins has been assigned to teach a continuing education course in the weekend college entitled "Mini Computers for the Small Business." And in a midwestern liberal arts college, Bernice Alton has just concluded an interview with a forty-two-year-old corporate personnel specialist who is seeking credit for prior learning. These three faculty from different institutions have one thing in common. By design or circumstance, they are part of the growing faculty for the lifelong learner.

A Game of Numbers

During the past few years there has been much discussion about lifelong learners and the impact that they have had and potentially can have on American higher education. On some campuses, older students already outnumber the typical eighteen- to twenty-two-year-olds, and demographers and educational researchers tell us that this trend will continue. Not only are adult learners swelling college classrooms, but they are availing themselves of all other kinds of sponsored and self-directed learning opportunities.

24

In addition to these data on adult learners, we are also aware of the diminishing pool of eighteen- to twenty-two-year-old students. In 1973, the U.S. Census Bureau reported that in 1980 the rising number of eighteen-year-old people will crest and will then sharply decline for a ten-year period, each year reducing the potential high school graduates upon which colleges and universities, until recently, had to depend to fill their classrooms (see Figure 1). Changes in the military draft, increased employment opportunities, and disenchantment about the true value of a college degree have further reduced the number of eighteen- to twenty-two-year olds for colleges. Because institutional budgets and faculty loads are most often built on the number of students served, there is continual pressure to maintain or to increase enrollment. The declining number of younger people and the increasing quest by adults for learning alternatives pose an invitation to college and university teachers to become more intensively involved in the prospect of being the faculty for the lifelong learner.

But this invitation carries certain responsibilities on the part of the faculty member, responsibilities that affect policies, the content of their curriculum, and their teaching methods.

A Need for a New Orientation

Last week an old friend whom we had not seen for several years, upon seeing our children, commented: "Somehow they've changed. I guess they're taller." This observation is not unlike our response to teaching the adult stu-

Figure 1. Persons 18–21 Years Old (in thousands)

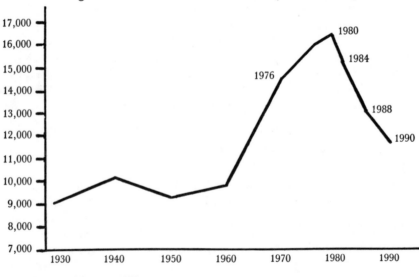

Source: Bureau of Census, 1973

dent. Quite often they are treated as older versions of the eighteen- to twenty-two-year-old when, in reality, adult learners are quite different (Gross, 1977). Their perspective on life is different. They have a different sense of themselves, their time, of what's worth learning, and how they intend to use their learning.

If we can agree that the differences between adult and youthful learners go beyond an age differential and that these differences are important considerations in structuring a teaching/learning process, then it is important to examine these characteristics and the implications that they have for teaching.

Understanding Why They Come

The reasons for adults to seek college and to participate in a formal education activity may be highly diverse. However, each adult has a reason that could be important to the faculty member who is orchestrating the learning environment. Some of the more common reasons motivating adults to enter college are to prepare for a new career, gain skills and knowledge that can be applied to a present career or occupation, to cope with personal or family concerns, to learn for learning's sake, and to simply complete a degree. Morstain and Smart (1973) reported that it may be possible to link an adult's reason for participation in higher education with learner typology. In a study that they conducted, 648 adult college students were classified on the basis of the *Education Participation Scale* as "Nondirected Learners," those with an undifferentiated pattern of motivational orientations or no specific goals or purpose; "Social Learners," those whose primary interest was with people and relationships; "Stimulation Seeking Learners," who want to escape from routine and boredom either in personal or occupational life by expanding horizons; "Career Oriented Learners," who see learning as directly related and important to their career or occupation, carefully weighing potential benefits and outcomes; and lastly, those that might be called "Life Change Learners," those that see education as a way to alter several aspects of their life—perhaps to give it new direction.

If faculty can develop an understanding for the reasons that a person has elected to pursue an educational activity, it can have important implications for the way they choose to structure the teaching/learning environment. For example, the people who are in college for occupational reasons, perhaps to learn new skills that they need in order to maintain or to advance in their job, will probably respond best if they can see clear utility and application of what they are learning. On the other hand, a person who has come for the "joy of learning" may respond to a more theoretical format emphasizing philosophy, ideas, and issues. And a person who has enrolled to gain knowledge and skills to help cope with personal or family concerns may respond best to a teaching situation that emphasizes group discussions, stimulation, and feedback. Therefore, what motivates adults to enroll in a college or university can also affect the extent and level of their participation and the benefits that they might receive. The more we know about the adult learner in terms of why they are here and how they learn, the better equipped we will be to develop appropriate programs, courses, and experiences.

The Adult as a Learner

All adults are involved in lifelong learning as they move through life stages, adjust to new roles, face life crises, and undertake new opportunities. Although much of this learning is global and diffuse (Knox, 1977), nearly every adult engages in some kind of extended learning project each year (Tough, 1977). What's more, Tough also found that many of these adults were learning at an exceptionally high level.

Even with the enormous involvement that adults have with lifelong learning, however, their learning styles and characteristics affecting them as learners change. In the classic text, *Adult Development and Learning,* Knox identified the following seven modifiers to adult learning:

1. Condition: Physiological condition and physical health can affect learning and cognition in various ways. Sensory impairment, such as poor vision or hearing loss, can restrict sensory input. Inadequate cerebral circulation or stress can impair memory. Ill health can restrict attention given to external events.
2. Adjustment: The effective facilitation of learning is less likely when there is substantial personal or social maladjustment in the learning situation.
3. Relevance: The adult's motivation and cooperation in the learning activity is more likely when the tasks are meaningful and of interest to the learner.
4. Speed: Especially for older adults, time limits and pressures tend to reduce learning performance.
5. Status: Socioeconomic circumstances are associated with values, demands, constraints, and resources that can affect learning ability. Level of formal education tends to be a status index most highly associated with adult learning.
6. Change: Social change can create substantial differences between older and younger age cohorts (such as two generations) regarding the experience and values internalized during childhood and adolescence.
7. Outlook: Personal outlook and personality characteristics, such as openmindedness or defensiveness, can affect the way in which an adult deals with specific types of learning situations.

In addition to these conditions that potentially modify adult learning, there are several other factors that faculty should be sensitive to in teaching the lifelong learner (Wimette, 1977).

Some adults are doubtful about their ability to learn. Having been away from formal education, they are sometimes afraid of the competition presented by the younger "sharper" student. To minimize this concern, faculty should avoid situations where they compare learners, deal with academic and personal problems of the learner in private, use positive reinforcement, assist students, identify mechanisms to understand and measure their progress, and be alert for other indicators of insecurity.

A second characteristic of adults as learners is that they have many more experiences to draw upon than younger students. The awareness of these experiences can serve as a rich resource for the faculty member to better understand the learner in terms of past experiences, present activities, and future plans. In one institution a faculty member has developed a personal information sheet that students fill out at the beginning of each semester. The purpose of this is to identify information and experiences that he can use to help guide his instructional plan, taking into consideration the personal needs and experiences of those in his class.

A third characteristic is that participation in an emotional activity may be a second or third level priority for lifelong learners. In addition to being students, they often have job, family, and other personal circumstances that interfere with their academic functions. One veteran adult educator expressed his approach as loose and flexible, citing examples of arranging in-place-of-class learning activities for the mother who had to stay at home for an extended period with a sick child, make up assignments for the salesman who was regularly out of town, and curricular and material modification to accommodate specific learning needs. Like this faculty member, others who have become involved with the teaching of adult learners have found that they need to be extremely sensitive to the personal circumstances of adults that affect their involvement in educational activities.

To provide the experiences and the environment appropriate for the lifelong learners requires a commitment on the part of the graduate schools who are preparing our future faculty, the institutions that faculty are serving in, and the individual faculty members who are ultimately responsible for their own professional skills.

The Role of the Graduate School

Few graduate schools prepare their students for teaching in any practical sense, leaving classroom performance largely to chance. Even fewer graduate institutions prepare future faculty for teaching lifelong learners. Elementary and secondary educators have long known that it takes more than content knowledge to be a successful teacher and have built into the teacher training programs instruction on learning theory, child development, and teaching methods. Yet when it comes to college faculty, the Ph.D. or content knowledge become the entry criteria. Seldom does one have an opportunity to study adult development and adult teaching techniques prior to entering the class-room.

With the extent of adults participating in higher education, graduate insti-tutions have a responsibility to expand their preparatory programs to teach the skills and entry level competencies that faculty will need for teaching the lifelong learner. In addition they should routinely have available short term work-shops, summer institutes, and continuing education programs that develop and enhance the skills and competencies of the teachers of the lifelong learner.

The Role for Institutional In-Service

Almost every institution has some provision for in-service faculty development. The range of these efforts is from modest, low-cost programs to complex models of organizational development. Although the worth and suc-cess of faculty development activities may be a debatable issue, faculty remain the number one resource of an institution. Their ability to function effectively and efficiently will determine more than any other factor how well the institu-tional goals will be achieved. One cannot assume that the faculty enter an institution prepared to serve the educational needs of the lifelong learner. Content knowledge and prior experience with younger learners are inade-quate preparation for the task of teaching older adults. Therefore, if the insti-tution is in the business of lifelong learning, then there is a place for profes-sional development and in-service activities designed to develop and to improve the professional skills for faculty serving this clientele.

Some examples of institutional efforts in providing professional oppor-tunities include tuition reimbursement for graduate course work related to the adult learner, expenses for workshops and conferences on adult learning, cam-pus programs on techniques of teaching adults, and professional materials, subscriptions, and sabbaticals that focus on the lifelong learner.

Other institutions include program development as part of their faculty in-service activities and provide opportunities for faculty to develop new and innovative programs dealing with lifelong learning. An example of this type of activity could be the employment of consultants and releasing time to enable a faculty committee to implement a program for adults to receive college credit for experiential learning.

Those institutions that employ the concept of organizational develop-ment recognize the necessity to structure staff development throughout the institution to include faculty, administrators, and classified staff. Through this organizational thrust the institution would develop admission policies, coun-seling services, instructional program, and extracurricular activities that are consistent with the needs and interest of the lifelong learner. In addition, all faculty, administrators, and staff would participate in professional develop-ment activities designed to equip them with the skills and competencies neces-sary to function within their roles in serving the adult learner.

Self-Assessment and Self-Directed Growth

In spite of the fact that we have charged graduate institutions and directors of college in-service activities to become more responsible for the development of the faculty for the lifelong learner, it is ultimately all teachers' personal obligation for their own professional growth. As lifelong learners themselves, they could become students of adult learning and development. By identifying the skills that are needed, faculty members could then identify how they learn, what they need to learn, and what resources are available. Through this process they can then structure a self-directed educational plan to develop and strengthen their teaching competencies.

Conclusion

Several conclusions can be made, some specific and definite, others more general and obscure. It is quite obvious that the future of American higher education will be greatly affected by the emergence of the lifelong learner and by the decreasing availability of the eighteen- to twenty-two-year-old students. The reasons that are motivating these older students to enter college will be as diverse as their educational backgrounds and learner characteristics. Yet it is the faculty member's responsibility to create a learning environment and to guide the educational experiences suitable for their needs.

To develop the skills and the competencies that faculty will need for this task has to be shared: shared by the graduate training programs, the employing institutions and the individual faculty member. Perhaps the challenge of preparing faculty for the lifelong learner is awesome or at least troublesome; nevertheless, the consequences of not doing so are even more awesome.

References

Gross, R. *The Lifelong Learner.* New York: Simon & Schuster, 1977.

Knox, A. B. *Adult Development and Learning: A Handbook on Individual Growth and Competence in the Adult Years for Education and the Helping Professions.* San Francisco: Jossey-Bass, 1977.

Morstain, B., and Smart, J. "A Motivational Typology of Adult Learners." *Journal of Higher Education, 48* (6), 665–679.

Tough, A. *The Adults Learning Project.* Toronto, Canada: Ontario Institute for Studies in Education, 1977.

Wimette, D. C. *The Problem of Adult Learners.* (Project 309.) Chicago: Illinois Office of Education, 1977.

Frank Christensen formerly served as director of William Rainey Harper College's nontraditional degree program. He currently serves as a regional manager for the Council for the Advancement of Experiential Learning.

*A developmental counseling program can make the difference between
success and failure as reentry adults, making important changes
and decisions, test their ability to achieve.*

Counseling for Development

G. Richard Eisele

Wonderful things don't always happen when adult learners are plugged into
existing classes, significant developmental and critical life changes don't stop
happening after the early twenties. In fact, the adult transitions may be
equally as meaningful and problematic as the adolescent transitions (Gould,
1975). Reentry into education itself clearly indicates movement, decisions
being made, and transitions in progress. For some returning students, college
may be the testing ground for what Erikson (1963) calls "generativity versus
stagnation" issues: "Am I really capable of becoming more than I am?", "Will I
be able to learn at the college level?", "Will I be able to go to school and keep
my family and job intact?"

These can be times of uncertainty and self-reflection, times when some
of the old questions of personal value and worth are reevaluated. There is a
natural apprehension over returning to school often intensified by a fear of
failure based on negative past experiences. And yet there can be a level of optimism and faith that almost defies analysis. Many believe that this new adventure will provide opportunities for increased fulfillment, productivity, and
self-expression (Muskat, 1978).

That very optimism, however, contains the seeds for future discouragement. Fear of failure and willingness to take new risks are often in delicate
balance, with each experience having the potential to disrupt that balance for
better or worse.

Many of us have experienced, and current research confirms, that
adult learners appear to be in a hurry to get somewhere and often set rather

unrealistic goals. There seems to be a sense that time left to learn and grow is limited. This impatience is often in conflict with a lack of basic skills and a confusion about available career and educational opportunities. Time and time again, older students come in with an elevated career goal, a desire for an associate degree, and little awareness of the need for writing skills. It is a great frustration for them to have to take the time to learn to write.

It is imperative that we temper our eagerness to seek lifelong learners as clients with an equal sense of responsibility for serving them well. Some will make it almost in spite of what we do. We can rather easily meet the expectations of the professional looking for career advancement, the middle class housewife looking for new friends and a new hobby, and the small business owner in need of accounting skills. It is the students who are not quite so clear of purpose, not as self-confident, and not quite so well informed who need more than just a course menu (Sawhill, 1978). Without a thorough self-assessment and without an understanding of available offerings, they will be unable to integrate program with need. Poor choices will be made and some may leave with less confidence than when they came. Failure experiences for reentry students can often lead to complete discouragement, damaged self-concepts, and avoidance of future learning opportunities.

Program Functions

To effectively meet the needs of these students, counseling is as essential as contract learning, flexible scheduling, decentralized locations, assessment of prior learning, developmental skills offerings, and other programmatic responses to the new clientele. Counseling functions can be integrated with other programs but they must be provided and directed primarily toward the students most in need.

Academic Advisement. One of the prime functions of a good counseling program is to provide guidance in the process of academic planning and participation. Knowles (1972) and other educators have shown that adults have immediate short term goals and a problem-centered orientation to learning. Very often this takes the form of career and vocational concerns. They want relevance between their educational experiences and their immediate career goals. They want each course to have immediate usefulness. However, beneath this surface concern hide some of the aforementioned anxieties, confusion, and uncertainties about their lives in general (Nash and Saurman, 1978). Counseling can enhance self-understanding and help students make some sense out of and find meaning in a complex array of educational opportunities. Often unifying themes and sequences can be found that pertain to a broader view of self and to those immediate goals. The adult student who wants to be a small business administrator may discover that poor interpersonal skills are the weak links both in terms of her personal life and her vocational aspirations. The prospective social worker may find new value and meaning in the study of history and culture.

Decision Making. Making better choices involves knowing more about oneself and about the options available, but the greatest payoff may be that by making better choices students will feel more effective as people (Nelson, 1976). The counseling program should help students become better planners and evaluators of their own learning. It should work to promote the psychological principle of movement from dependence to independence or self-reliance. Learners can become better self-assessors, planners, participants, and evaluators with practice and more awareness of what it is they are doing and learning.

Learning Skills. As students get involved in academic experiences, a concomitant counseling process can help them discover and develop information processing skills that can be used in any learning situation. Analyzing the similarities and differences among African cultures and comparing Freudian and Rogerian theories of psychology basically require the same cognitive skills. By learning to compare and contrast, synthesize and analyze, students can enrich their experience with each content area selected.

The Environment. To accomplish these tasks, it is essential to create a supportive and encouraging environment where personal, career, and educational goals can be explored and where students can develop the skills and confidence necessary to take responsibility for their own growth and development. Encouragement and support does not mean the overuse of sympathy and praise. Although some praise can be used effectively, excess use can lead to student dependency and distrust.

The tension that results from the coexistence of a willingness to take risks and a fear of failure can lead to student growth. We cannot and should not remove all the risks and challenges inherent in this new adventure. However, we can demonstrate that success often comes in small increments, emphasize the value of small gains, and cushion the jolt of reality. Students should be guided into learning experiences that are slightly beyond their present capacities so that growth rather than discouragement is the result (Cross, 1971). We can also keep failure in perspective by using peer support, paying attention to individual strengths, and examining the learning that can result from unsuccessful experiences. "Even though you didn't finish the work for that course, your determined attitudes and the results of your project were great," and "You know, Mary, I have the same problems writing things down that you have" are the kinds of encouraging remarks often heard in a developmental counseling program.

Liaison. It is important to keep in mind that a counseling program cannot be all things for all students. Without enlightened administrators and faculty, a strong developmental skills program, and some of the programmatic arrangements mentioned earlier, results will not be satisfactory. The program, however, can be a conduit through which information can flow to and from the faculty and the administration. Increased knowledge of the concerns, needs, and idiosyncrasies of adult learners can be communicated to instructors and administrators and in turn information about the college and its faculty can be shared with students. This mutuality of understanding and flow of information is necessary if the different parts of the college are to work as a consortium for serving the lifelong learner.

Referrals. The program also should act as a referral and brokering agency to resources both within and outside the college. Needs will arise during the planning process that cannot be met by the counseling program or the regular curriculum. One of the needs certain to emerge is for a strong developmental skills program. As we all know, many otherwise competent and intelligent students are lacking in language, mathematical, or study skills. Ideally, the counseling program can identify and refer these students to appropriate resources before they get involved with too many learning experiences that require those skills.

In-depth personal, career, or psychotherapeutic counseling is most likely beyond the capabilities of the college. Trying to meet student needs in these areas would undoubtedly be at the expense of other students. The counseling program can refer those students to mental health and other appropriate service providers.

The Counselor-Instructor

So far we have viewed counseling as a process rather than the behavior of a person. However, the vital core, the sine qua non, of any program resides in the people staffing it. To implement the above functions effectively, the counselor-instructor must have a firm belief in the potential of all students to grow and develop. This should be combined with individual and group facilitation skills, the ability to relate with faculty and administrators, and a solid understanding of the institution, other available programs, and their effect on student development. Working with adult students requires the ability to help students assess needs, values, styles, and goals and to translate those needs into an educational plan. At the risk of painting an almost quixotic picture, the counselor should have both the knowledge of cognitive processes and the ability to demonstrate how skills gained in one experience can be used in other learning situations. This is a person who is more generalist than specialist, as much a teacher as a counselor. Familiarity with the stages, developmental tasks, and differing learning styles of adults is another prerequisite along with the ability to lead students through a process of inquiry. For example, some learners will have a rather simple view of the world, seeing things as "rights and wrongs" or "blacks and whites." They will identify with authority figures and accept their definitions of right and wrong. Others will be much more tentative in their assessments and complex in their thinking. They may seek more independence and less structure in their learning environments. Some students may really learn something only when they have practiced it; others will learn better from reading, writing, and reflective observation. The counselor must be able to help students become familiar with their own uniqueness and help them plan experiences that are congruent with yet challenging to their present condition.

Whether or not a program is successful may ultimately rest with the attitudes of its staff. Counselor-instructors should have a high tolerance for ambiguity and a willingness to risk involvement; they are not afraid to encounter others or themselves (O'Banion and others, 1970). Because attitudes seem to be contagious, the chief ingredient for the educational counselor may be an enthusiasm for life and learning.

Alternative Arrangements

Since the counseling process is so necessary in the educational development of many lifelong learners, we will have to find innovative alternatives to the costly and sometimes ineffective "counselor in cubicle" model. Very few institutions these days have the luxury of hiring a large staff to meet the needs of a new group of students. Some of the alternatives used successfully include: the establishment of decentralized learning centers where students can drop in for personalized service; the use of educational mentors who provide both guidance and instruction as a student moves through an academic program; the use of adjunct counselors as supplements to an already overburdened staff; the use of telephone counseling services for home-based learners; and the development of life, career, and academic planning workshops that run parallel to the students' other courses.

A Proposed Model

I would like to briefly propose a developmental counseling model for adult learners. It is a model that closely resembles the one used at the Community College of Vermont. The settings are groups of between eight and fifteen students. The agenda is learner assessment and educational planning with peer interaction, support, encouragement, reality orientation, and the development of self-reliance as themes in counterpoint. The counselor-instructor facilitates support and interaction, provides information, and teaches learning process skills. An important adjunct component is a set of materials, a handbook or workbook, that provides assessment information and exercises, descriptions of available college programs, and aids for implementing and evaluating learning activities. The materials may be used by individuals to supplement the group activities or as a textbook-like resource for the class.

The environment for students is characterized as both supportive and challenging. The learner is in a state of moderate tension where he is challenged to extend slightly beyond his present level of development; the dualistic thinker, for instance, who sees only two extremes possible can be encouraged to explore a range of intermediate alternatives. Opportunities are provided for students to alternate between self-reflective and active participant modes. Students are encouraged to discover new things about themselves and to apply those understandings by trying out new activities and behaviors both within and outside of the counseling group. The resultant new learning is then reflected on, evaluated, and integrated with prior knowledge and skills.

In the ideal situation, this process is the student's first experience with the college. It should begin before extensive involvement with the regular curriculum takes place. However, it is more than orientation. It provides an ongoing support group for the student as other academic content areas are explored.

Because this process encourages cognitive growth and development, and because the learner is becoming more proficient as a consumer of and participant in educational opportunities, this experience is central to the needy student's academic program.

Stages. The model is developmental because it progresses in stages. Learning and attitudes from one stage form the basis for the next and the success of each stage is to a large degree dependent on the success of the prior stage. We have described the stages as assessment, planning, implementation, and evaluation. These labels should not be viewed as tight, exclusive categories of activities but as a useful framework to help students understand the sequences within the process as a whole. One cannot plan effectively without assessing the present situation, and implementing a faculty plan will usually be less than satisfactory. The evaluation stage allows for reflection on new learning gained and provides information useful for future assessment activities.

Its application in practice can be briefly described as follows: it is in the assessment stage that many of the myriad dimensions of individual differences are explored. Exercises, activities, written materials, and instruments are used to help students increase their self-awareness around such topics as learning and interpersonal styles, values, present knowledge and skills, and personal, career and educational goals. Increased self-understanding and new skills for self-reflection are developed. Students in need of special diagnostic testing are referred to the proper resources. This stage provides the foundation, the groundwork, from which all other activities are built.

Once this information has been organized so that it is understandable to the student and to others, the planning process begins. Information about available learning options is juxtaposed with knowledge gained from the assessment stage. It is here that students often become aware of some unforeseen realities (such as lack of requisite skills and knowledge, ambitiousness of goals, anticipated opportunities not available). New awareness of strengths, on the other hand, produces a higher level of self-confidence and motivation. Students develop decision and choice making skills as they weigh the advantages and disadvantages of various options against their more clearly defined goals.

The implementation stage involves helping students get the most out of their chosen learning experiences. Through role playing, discussion, written exercises and materials, active involvement is emphasized along with the development of cognitive and learning process skills.

Evaluation ideally occurs throughout the process but becomes the dominant theme near the end of each cycle. Students reflect on such questions as: "To what extent am I accomplishing my goals?", "What new knowledge and skills am I acquiring?", "How well am I learning them?", and "What am I learning that I didn't plan for?"

Throughout this cycle, channels of communication are kept open with instructors and administrators and appointments for individual counseling or referrals to other programs are made when necessary.

It is important to reaffirm that if the process is successful, learners will be more independent and self-reliant. They will make the best possible use of available resources. An awareness of limitations will be offset by increased self-confidence and enthusiasm. They will understand and handle the learning process better. In essence, they will be more effective, less dependent consumers of education.

Conclusion

Of course, the contents of this chapter can only scratch the surface of what a good counseling program should be. Any institution serving lifelong learners will have to sets it own objectives and from those derive the most appropriate functions and activities. The actual model designed will have to mesh with the needs and constraints of the college and of the students served. What does seem clear is that mere caveat emptors in the catalogue will not suffice.

The lifelong learning movement holds great promise both for the growth of the participating adults and for the vigor of the institutions involved. The absence of support programs for these students is as likely as watered down curriculums and lack of standards to prevent us from keeping that promise.

References

Cross, K. P. *Beyond the Open Door: New Students to Higher Education*. San Francisco: Jossey-Bass, 1971.

Erikson, E. H. *Childhood and Society*. New York: Norton, 1963.

Gould, R. "Adult Life Stages: Growth Toward Self-Tolerance," *Psychology Today*, 1975, *8* (9), 74–78.

Knowles, M. S. *The Modern Practice of Adult Education* New York: Association Press, 1975.

Muskat, H. S. "Women Re-Entering College: Some Basic Ingredients for Curriculum Development." *Personnel and Guidance Journal*, 1978, *57* (3), 153–156.

Nash, R. J., and Saurman, K. P. "Learning to Earn Is Not Learning To Live: Student Development Educators as Meaning Makers." *Personal and Guidance Journal,* 1978, *57* (2), 84–89.

Nelson, R. C. "Choice Awareness: An Unlimited Horizon." *Personnel and Guidance Journal,* 1976, *54* (9), 463–467.

O'Banion, T., Thurston, A., and Gulden, J. "Student Personnel Work: An Emerging Model." *Junior College Journal,* 1970, *41* (3), 7–14.

Sawhill, J. C. "Lifelong Learning: Scandal of the Next Decade?" *Change Magazine,* 1978/ 1979, *10* (11), 7, 80.

G. Richard Eisele is a learning services coordinator for the Community College of Vermont (CCV). For the past three years he has also been directing a Kellog funded project where collaboration among six institutions is used to improve the teaching-learning process for CCV adults. He has many years of experience counseling and teaching people of all ages.

Various types of competence-based programs focus attention on educational outcomes, evaluate practices on the basis of performance, improve the credentialing process, offer flexibility, and provide quality control of educational experiences.

Competence-Based Education for Adult Learners

E. Sharon Hayenga
Hope B. Isaacson

The concepts of competence-based education and adult learners both defy straightforward characterization. Adult learners, who are attending colleges and universities in unprecedented numbers, have not enrolled for higher education with a discrete or homogeneous set of characteristics, abilities, or needs. Likewise, competence-based education is a very complex educational concept; and its complexity is compounded by the fact that it has been operationalized, and thus defined, idiosyncratically from program to program, and from school to school.

Competence-based education has enjoyed more attention during the 1970s than in the decades which preceded it. Secondary schools, as well as postsecondary institutions, are looking at competence evaluation as a potential solution to contentions of declining standards. Actually, many aspects of the Adult Basic Education projects and GED testing practices are competence-based ways of allowing adults to earn high school credentials; and many colleges and universities have either considered developing programs in competence-based education, or have already implemented such programs, in response to the concern for more meaningful credentials and to the social justice arguments of adults.

Americans are particularly responsive to the connotations of competence-based education because of their esteem for competence: notions of innate individual competence, a valuing of each individual's rights to achieve, and the sense that all persons should have equality of access are ideas and values which have shaped the nation's most complex social policies, including education. It is this value system, in conjunction with the notion that social agencies are ultimately accountable to all citizens, which supports much of the kind of programming competence-based education might make possible: flexibility of access and pacing; fixed, nondiscriminatory standards; clarity; individualization, and others.

What Is Competence-Based Education?

It is difficult to generalize about competence-based education, because all education is, by implication, competence-based, and because there is tremendous programmatic variation among competence-based education programs. Some characteristics tend to transcend programmatic differences, however, and do distinguish competence-based education from more commonly practiced classroom instruction. Probably the most distinctive feature is that competence-based education focuses most of its attention on educational outcomes; such programs deemphasize the specialness of the classroom as an educational process and profess at least an egalitarian attitude toward a broad spectrum of educational processes. They argue that such flexibility best serves individual learning needs, and enhances long-term educational benefits.

Certainly competence-based education programs that are thoughtfully developed and are carefully implemented emphasize educational processes. The difference is that all the educational processes are focused toward the outcomes (competence). Thus the educational process becomes a means of achieving an end, rather than an end in itself.

Educational units in a competence-based program tend to be more discrete and much more explicit than traditional classroom work. Expected outcomes, instructional resources, teaching methods, and evaluation criteria and processes are articulated prior to the beginning of the unit. Ideally, such factors will remain constant — from classroom to classroom, and from the beginning to the end of the unit. They should serve to focus educational activity for the duration of study on any given competence.

Evaluation practices in a competence-based program tend toward performance tests, rather than paper and pencil tests. Ideally, performance measures will measure actual competence, as opposed to the mastery of the content. (Content mastery is often used as a proxy for competence, and the obvious shortcomings of such equivalency are strong forces supporting the competence-based education movement.) In addition to a preference for perfor-

mance evaluations, competence-based programs emphasize criterion referenced measures, rather than commonly used normative standards. Proponents argue the constant standards support both accountability and equality in
ways which are superior to more flexible normative standards.

Some Types of Competence-Based Programs

Fortunately, the concept of competence-based education is flexible.
Institutions have been able to adapt the basic principles to meet institution-
specific needs.

Alverno College, a liberal arts college in Milwaukee, has developed one of
the most widely respected and publicized competence-based education programs
in the United States. The college took a very sophisticated approach to con-
verting its entire undergraduate liberal arts curriculum to a competence-based
program for educating primarily first generation college women. It is one of a
very few programs which attempted to reconcile the philosophical tension
between competence-based education and the liberal arts by developing a two-
track program: the curriculum of the college features discipline-bound coursework (content), and offers, additionally, instructional resources which help
students achieve the broad, general competencies which the college has designated as the educational outcomes which its liberal arts degree represents.

Students' achievements are recorded on a two-track transcript, record-
ing progress both through the discipline-bound coursework of the college and
the required achievement levels of each of the eight competence areas: develop
effective communication skills; sharpen analytical abilities; develop a facility
for making value judgments and independent decisions; develop a facility for
social interaction; achieve an understanding of the relationship of the individual and the environment; develop an awareness and understanding of the
world in which the individual lives; develop knowledge, understanding, and
responsiveness to the arts, and knowledge and understanding of the humani-
ties; and develop workable problem-solving skills.

Assessment of the coursework and academic majors and minors is conducted by the faculty. Assessment of most of the competencies required in the
eight major competence areas is conducted primarily in a sophisticated, centralized assessment center which is staffed with both faculty and community
professionals.

A different kind of competence-based education program has been
designed by MANEC (Metropolitan Area Nursing Education Consortium).
It is a consortium effort, involving all five public postsecondary education
institutions in greater St. Paul, Minnesota—two vocational technical schools
(916, 917), which offer practical nursing programs; two community colleges
(Inver Hills, Lakewood), which offer associate degree registered nurse programs; and one baccalaureate institution (Metropolitan State University)
which offers a baccalaureate degree in nursing.

Their consortium model is focusing on the development of a competence-based vertically articulated career ladder program for nursing personnel. It features the standardized assessment of student competences in units which are much smaller than course equivalents, thereby maximizing the students' use of time, and also allowing licensed practical nurses to earn clearly articulated advanced standing in an associate degree nursing program, and allowing both LPNs and RNs the opportunity to earn advanced standing in the baccalaureate level nursing program. The competence-based approach has been designed to facilitate professional upgrading and new licensure requirements by focusing on competences rather than coursework or method of transcripting (for instance, vocational schools record LPN students' achievements in clock hours; the colleges record achievement in credit).

The educational institutions have together defined the competences which span the nursing profession from LPN to BSN. Their program allows flexible entry and flexible exit, and emphasizes the assignation of the nursing credential based on demonstrated performance against criterion referenced measures. Detailed records of student progress and student performance are on file, and evidence to date suggests that students' performance is high, both on the job and on state board examinations. The assessment of competences, as well as the instructional plans, emphasize the interpersonal and affective aspects of nursing, as well as the knowledge and skills aspects. There is substantial evidence to suggest that student performance is higher as a result of the competence-based program, and also that the articulated career ladder will have a very positive effect on the careers of many adult women who have worked for years as nurses' aids or licensed practical nurses.

Still another kind of competence program utilizes instructional technology, a component which offers maximum flexibility of access and individualization of pacing. Potentially, it may even reduce the cost of individualized instruction (once the equipment has been amortized). An example of this type of competence-based education is PLATO (Personalized Learning and Teaching Opportunity), a computerized instructional system developed by Control Data Corporation. Corporations, proprietary schools, community education centers, technical schools, libraries, and colleges use it to teach specific concepts and skills. To date, the PLATO system offers a wide variety of programs, ranging from courses in composition and financial management to resume writing and blackjack (it is possible to play games with this computer for fun!).

The major drawback to technological teaching equipment is the rigidity of the system. While the programs typically measure competence and presume mastery, there is ample evidence to suggest that the equipment has very limited uses, primarily for individualized tutoring or supplemental education. There is no tolerance for individual learning styles, and there is only the most minimal support and feedback system.

Finally, many colleges have found a modified form of competence-based education to be the best approach for a program which credits prior experiential learning. The metropolitan area Minnesota community colleges developed a consortium program (which dropped most of the consortial dimensions once each of the individual programs became fully operational) for crediting prior experiential learning on the basis of demonstrated competence. The consortium features of the program met with difficulty in the face of each institution's sense of autonomy with regard to academic standards and curriculum. The administrative aspects of the colleges' programs remain uniform, however.

The six community colleges allow adults past the age of twenty-five to earn credit for prior learning by demonstrating competence in the academic areas which are taught by the collective colleges in Minnesota. Full-time faculty, part-time faculty, and community evaluators assist students in establishing the criteria for competence evaluation and in selecting an assessment technique which seems most suitable to the competence. The system has been designed as nonpunitive, in the sense that faculty assist students in preparing for competence evaluation by providing clear information about the competence, criteria and measurement techniques, and by offering suggestions for review reading or applied experience.

The programs articulate very well with existing programs at each of the colleges. Administrative policies have enabled the programs to be financially successful, and transfer and articulation policies which are favorable to the crediting of prior experiential learning have been worked out with most of the nearby baccalaureate level institutions. Most faculty express a clear preference for the competence-based approach which calls for a new measure of the students' competence, in contrast to the awarding of a block of credits for life experience learning, or to the evaluation of a complete student portfolio, both fairly common practices for the awarding of credit for prior experiential learning.

Why the Recent Emphasis on Competence-Based Education?

An implicit reason for the recent emphasis on competence-based education is probably, quite frankly, an increasing demand for new kinds and higher levels of competence. With increasing rates of both social and technological change, the shortcomings in an educational system which emphasizes single-setting applications of both thought and skills are disturbingly apparent. Focusing on competence, if it can be usefully and appropriately defined, offers the attractive prospect of more holistic and flexible educational programs.

In addition, proponents of competence-based education contend that it is the most workable approach to providing both the equality of access and the equality of outcome which many groups, previously educationally disadvantaged, need — most notably, women, ethnic minorities, employed adults, and persons who are working in occupations confronted with recently legislated position upgrading and relicensure standards. They see the explicitness of the competence-based system, as well as the inherent potential for individualization, as one of the best ways to end discrimination in education.

Many postsecondary schools are looking to competence-based education as one of the possible responses to charges of qualitative decline, and to demands from employers for some kind of performance quality control. Furthermore, it may offer the most viable alternative for attracting and retaining new student clienteles. A well-designed and carefully implemented competence-based education program has many connotations of integrity and of responsiveness, both important qualities in the minds of adult learners, and of skeptical first generation college students.

Some Problems Related to Managing Competence-Based Programs

Many issues in competence-based education remain unresolved. There are problems due to the lack of technical skill in competence articulation and measurement, and problems due to organizational processes and change. Faculty, particulary from fine schools with highly cherished traditions of individual academic autonomy, often resist a shift in emphasis from the process oriented system to the outcomes oriented system. Many also experience dismay at the new kinds of collegial relationships within the institution which must be developed before complete credentials can be defined and articulated.

Most academicians have not been trained in competence articulation, nor in measurement and evaluation. They are not practiced in seeing the interrelationships which often exist in the best competence programs. They often express concern that the focus on so much technical and process related information will rob learning of its vitality and will reduce minds from the creative to the literal. There is also widespread concern that competence training might become too career oriented, and that students will become too focused on functional aspects to the exclusion of aesthetic or cognitive insights. Many are concerned that the rigorous attention to defining outcomes, and levels of outcomes, will further stratify an already too complex and stratified system.

One of the most critical obstacles to the development and operation of any alternative program, including competence-based education, is the lack of leadership from within the system. Governing organizations and funding agencies have been slow to acknowledge the complexity and scope of the problems which higher education is having in its relationship with "new clienteles." Inadequate support and leadership will almost certainly mean that an inferior competence-based education program will be put in place. Such an unfortunate circumstance may be very self-defeating; it can easily reduce the vitality of the curriculum to a lifeless grid, seriously disrupt the organizational harmony of the institution, and disappoint once again the students for whom the program was designed. The implementation of a respectable competence-based education program almost certainly requires a rather substantial, long-term commitment.

Potential Contributions of a Competence-Based Program

Visionaries and proponents of competence-based education are quick to identify a number of very desirable contributions which such programs might make to higher education. One of the primary advantages is that it might improve the credentialing process, thereby restoring public confidence in the area of credentials and in the processes by which one acquires them.

There is the possibility that competence-based education offers the most workable option for providing the kinds of holistic definitions of competence which are so badly needed. Concurrently, it may be possible to design evaluation techniques which will measure actual competence, rather than proxies for competence.

A competence-based approach to crediting prior experiential learning may be the best alternative to achieve quality control over such practices, and may also be the most desirable approach for relating cooperative education, experiential learning, and advanced placement to the complete programs and curriculums of an advanced institution. Furthermore, a competence-based, individually paced program may be the most human and serviceable solution to the problems of students who learn more slowly or quickly than average.

Focusing on competence, rather than on educational processes, offers the advantage of integrating higher education more completely into the social fabric of the community. It paves the way for improved cooperative relationships with corporations, service organizations, and cultural institutions, because of the nondiscriminatory attention to educational outcome rather than process. The clear articulation of educational outcomes, and the consistent reporting of actual student performance are basic prerequisites to improved transfer relationships, a problem which is rapidly approaching the critical stage.

Finally, the development and implementation of a competence-based education program offers institutions an exciting opportunity for self-scrutiny and renewal. The involvement of new student clienteles brings richness to an academic community and greatly enhances the relationship of the organization to its external constituents. There is the additional benefit of improved student self-image.

Evidence about competence-based education programs is inconclusive, for the most part, except in two areas: (1) evidence does suggest that the programs can attract significant numbers of new learners and meet their needs well, at least in specific areas; and (2) students report an increased sense of self-worth and personal strength.

Summary

Competence-based education does offer the prospect of genuine educational reform. There are serious limitations, however; attempts to define holistic competence and to measure such complete aspects of competence have been only partially successful. While it is possible for competence-based education to make a number of significant educational contributions, there is also the possibility that it can give the illusion of reform without seriously impacting the problems it has been designed to address. Careful attention to the definitions of competence, to the implementation of assessment, and to the integration of the programs are necessary if such pitfalls are to be avoided.

However, evidence suggests that many students benefit from competence programs, particularly if such units complement a program which incorporates a variety of educational approaches. Adult learners, particularly, seem to respond well to the self-discipline required for competence-based programs, and there is overwhelming evidence to indicate that such students will increasingly insist on credit for experiential learning on a competence documentation basis.

The credentialing process, whether it be in the form of state-issued credentials or institutionally awarded certificates and degrees, is increasingly attacked for its discriminatory and superficial evaluation practices. This area stands to be improved greatly with a sophisticated competence-based evaluation process.

E. Sharon Hayenga is the director of Competence-Based Education at Inver Hills Community College, a metropolitan area Minnesota community college.

Hope B. Isaacson is associate dean in charge of occupational programs at that same college. Together they own Hayenga-Isaacson Associates, an educational consulting company.

Versatile outreach programs, effective media usage, special orientation and admission procedures, satellite centers, and individualized support systems can do much to recruit adults to college and to eliminate the town-gown disparity.

Approaches to Recruiting the Adult Learner

Linda Reisser

It is estimated that although the number of eighteen- to twenty-one-year-old students attending college will decline significantly during the next twenty years, the number of persons over twenty-five and seeking higher education will increase from 11 million to 22 million in 1990 (Weathersby, 1977). The projected enrollment shifts will also produce much more diversity among students. Students will differ from each other in increasingly significant ways. They will be high and low academic achievers, old and young, eager to earn vocationally oriented degrees quickly, and flexible in their desire to acquire knowledge for its own sake.

Cross, who has described these new learners in recent books and articles, has emphasized that the reservoir of new students increasingly includes those who are academically and financially disadvantaged. These students are more likely to be first generation college students, female, handicapped by inadequate verbal and written skills, inclined to be passive in learning situations, less interested in intellectual pursuits, and fearful of failure (Cross, 1971).

Those of us who have worked with older learners have seen other patterns. Many adults interested in returning to school:

1. Are easily frustrated by the language, procedures, and requirements of higher educational institutions;

2. Are excited about learning and highly motivated, but anxious about their abilities to compete with younger students;
3. Either have very specific career goals, or are at a loss to know how to relate their abilities and aptitudes to the job market;
4. Are unaware of the variety of nontraditional learning options available, such as independent study, individualized degree programs, credit for prior learning;
5. Have job and family responsibilities which complicate their academic schedules;
6. Are often at a turning point in their lives, such as a career change, transition from married to single life, or returning to school after a period of homemaking or part-time work;
7. Are easily alienated by institutional practices which fail to recognize their life experience, diverse learning styles and skills, needs to use time efficiently and to "personalize" their education, and special needs for child care services, basic learning skills, support groups, and extracurricular activities which appeal to adults;
8. Are making significant investments of time and money in order to accomplish educational goals.

Colleges and universities that wish to open their doors to more adult learners cannot continue to structure their recruitment and admission procedures as they have in the past. Some institutions that have been serving diverse adults have learned and benefited from adaptation, while others continue to follow tradition. It is not easy to examine and revamp outreach programs, or to reeducate faculty and staff, but it must be done if the real needs of adult learners are to be served.

Recruitment Techniques

Admission officials have routinely traveled to high schools and college transfer programs in order to contact potential students. Yet their approach to nontraditional students has been to wait for them to walk in and inquire, expect them to decode college catalogues and course schedules, and find their way around the alien environment of the campus.

To recruit more effectively, colleges must be creative in attracting the attention of lifelong learners, proactive in translating academic jargon into practical language, and conscientious about making adult learners feel comfortable and confident.

Publications should be revised or designed to appeal to lifelong learners. Pictures of adult learners with "testimonials" can speak more clearly to some audiences than a catalogue. Brochures should deal with frequently asked questions, such as "How do I register for courses?", "Can I be a full-time student and still keep my job?", "Can I get college credit for what I already know?", "What about health care and financial aid?" Services must be described with the adult learner in mind.

Special interest courses, workshops, and forums can be designed for specific groups and brought off campus to the community. Adults may initially feel more inclined to attend an evening discussion on marriage and divorce than a semester-long sociology course on "The Changing Family." Yet one can be used to stimulate interest in the other. Short courses, brown bag lunch seminars, and one day workshops provide contact points for faculty and community members. They portray college staff as a group of credible people, interested in current topics, approachable and exciting. Furthermore, they reinforce the notion that learning is a useful and enjoyable pastime for all ages.

Outreach courses are especially appropriate for adults if they are designed to address their real life problems, such as relating to others, parenting, life cycle changes, managing money, health, and diet, energy conservation or various self-improvement tools. Books like Gail Sheehy's *Passages* have stimulated interest in various life stages, and highlighted the fact that adults in different stages have different interests, crises, and developmental tasks. Courses aimed at each life stage may have more appeal than traditional topics in the social sciences.

Other successful offerings may deal with practical skills for upward mobility, such as management skills, public speaking, financial planning, crisis intervention, assertiveness training or the latest techniques in a trade or profession. Still others appeal to popular interests, such as psychic phenomena, UFOs, gourmet cooking, popular films or books, organic gardening, regional or local issues, and political, cultural, or social developments like the women's movement or the antinuclear power demonstrations.

Continuing education programs have been doing these kinds of things for years. But sometimes academic administrators fail to see their potential for turning workshop participants into full-time students and therefore do not suggest any followup. How many academic departments take time to brainstorm ideas for creative educational offerings based on the interests of adults in their community?

Courses designed for specific target groups have also proved successful at bringing new audiences into the university. South Dakota State University brought 300 senior citizens to the campus to sample minicourses in Scandinavian History, South Dakota Pioneers, Living on a Fixed Income, and Nutrition and Exercise. They also participated in a crafts fair and were provided with musical entertainment. Members of the Student Senate served as hosts. Based on the success of that one day program, an advisory council was formed to make the educational needs of senior citizens known to university officials, and plans were made for them to educate others about the experience of aging through use of the campus radio station.

Versatile outreach people who can elicit the educational needs of target groups can do a great deal to bridge the gap between town and gown. Workshops on management skills for women who work in financial institutions, empathy skills training for ministers, basic survival skills for the handicapped, pollution control and safety workshops for refinery employees, cardiopulmonary resuscitation for hospital personnel, field trips to metropolitan museums or theatres for art or drama groups, discussions of best sellers for library fans, workshops on the treatment of rape victims for law enforcement officers, public relations courses for business people, and other endless possibilities can add vitality to a community, as well as increase the college's reservoir of potential students.

Use of the media is also essential for recruiting adults. Beyond the placement of newspaper ads and public service announcements about registration times, colleges should develop strategies for portraying their sensitivity to the needs of adult learners. They can encourage feature articles on the student mother who graduated along with her son. They can inform the press about innovative activities of faculty members who test solar energy units on local farms or run special seminars for school counselors. Public information officers can look for radio and television opportunities for staff persons to discuss new degree programs, nontraditional student services, an on-campus meeting of a national association, or a new research project which will help the community.

Using the media to bolster the college's image as a service oriented, enjoyable, down to earth human enterprise will add to the positive public feelings about it. The message should be "We have something exciting and useful to offer you," instead of "We are a costly and intimidating collection of scholars who teach esoteric subjects to your children."

Surveys of the educational interests of local adults can be another way to inform the college as well as promote it. They can generate names and addresses of adults expressing an interest in a course or degree, as well as find patterns of preferred times and topics, needed services, and demographic data about potential students. Attached to the survey can be a list of the courses offered in the evenings for the current semester, some relevant facts about the number of older students enrolled, how easy it is to enroll, and who to contact for assistance.

Administering a survey, like reporting on a new program, provides a reason for college staff to be out in the county instead of stuck in their offices. It increases the person to person contacts so important for recruitment. It also reinforces the "we're interested and responsive" message.

Surveys can be conducted in traditional random sample ways or, even better, delivered in person to community groups, businesses, or professional meetings. The college should not overlook its own employees as potential students, and their accessibility as survey participants. Surveys of educational interests, especially when done for community groups or professional organizations, should be promptly followed up with course offerings or workshops.

Scholarships for adult learners are another tool for recruitment. These can include special awards created through fundraising drives, or small fifty dollar awards donated by student organizations. Financial aid staff must work to articulate the new options for middle income families, as well as to support lobbying efforts which will make current federal programs more flexible.

Referrals from other organizations and institutions should be encouraged through ongoing regular contact initiated by college staff. Colleges and universities in the surrounding area should be made aware of the special services provided to nontraditional students. Other types of organizations which serve potential students should be cultivated as referral sources. These include state agencies serving low income and disadvantaged persons, churches, senior citizen organizations, women's groups, service clubs, and professional associations. An articulate spokesperson for the nontraditional student program should seek invitations to address these groups, and should take along brochures and catalogues.

Developing good personal relationships with well-placed professions can not only spread the word about the college, but can also lead to other unexpected benefits, such as CETA trainees or human service program interns attaching themselves to the institution as recruiters or advisors, or collaborative grantwriting projects springing from shared community service goals.

Telephone followups are an essential part of proactive outreach. Many adults who are hesitant to press for information will open up to a responsive staff person who contacts them. Any excuse will do. Names on surveys, workshop rosters, or slips of paper passed along by currently enrolled friends can legitimize a phone call by someone representing the dean of students, or the admissions office, and wondering "whether you wanted more information about our degree options," or "if you'd like to attend a question and answer session." Sincere words of support and encouragement have made the difference between a homemaker continuing to stay at home versus "taking that course I've always wanted to take."

Special orientation sessions have been used successfully by some colleges to offer an alternative to the "Bring your parents and tour the Residence Halls" sessions. For working adults, it makes sense to organize evening meetings, with child care provided, and advertised as an "Open House" (preferably with refreshments). Potential adult learners are sometimes put off by meetings that sound too formal or intimidating. They prefer to be informal, bring a friend, and listen to other adults with whom they can identify.

One midwestern university enrolled increasing numbers of nontraditional students by moving away from afternoon orientations, which presented overviews by student affairs people and deans of colleges, to evening open houses focusing primarily on other adult learners discussing their decisions to return to school. This was followed by small group discussions or individual advising by generalists with human relations skills. College personnel who talk *at* potential nontraditional students sometimes lose audience attention by describing majors and minors, while the adult is wondering whether he or she will be the only forty-year-old in class. The emotional barriers to re-entering college are as formidable as the abstract issues of how many credits equal a degree.

Satellite Centers have worked to bring the college to the community, and demonstrate the variety and applicability inherent in lifelong learning activities. Adults are more likely to talk to each other about good programs, and attend them, if they are offered at convenient times and places. Whatcom Community College in Bellingham, Washington, has resisted establishing a central campus in order to make education more accessible to adults in its service area. It maintains six centers and rents fifty other sites around the county. Courses and workshops can be offered according to the needs of specific communities, from aquaculture courses on the Lummi Indian Reservation to self-paced data processing skills in a downtown business laboratory. The college also encourages community groups to use its facilities for meetings, and individuals to design self-directed learning contracts whether or not they wish to complete degrees.

Easing the Re-Entry Process

When adults finally walk in the door of an admissions office, they are ready for entry level advising. How this is done can make the difference between attrition and retention. The experience of successful recruiters suggests that adults need more individualized assistance at the entry point than do traditional students who have the benefit of recent experiences in academic settings, and the elaborate support systems built into residence halls. However, once these adults "know the ropes," they are very capable of negotiating their way through the system.

If adult learners are alienated at the entry point, they will not as easily stay around and learn the system from other students. Instead they will drive home and report the insensitivities to their friends and neighbors. Conversely, superb entry level advising will be reported to other adults as further evidence of the college's growing commitment to diverse adults.

A staff person (or small group of persons) should be clearly designated as coordinator of outreach efforts and the first person to be contacted for admissions and problem solving. There are several reasons for this. The college ceases to be an impersonal bureaucracy when there is at least one person who understands, helps, and advises in a consistent way, and to whom adults may refer others and know they will get results. This should be a trained professional with a commitment to adult learners, and a willingness to take people around to various offices, answer all pertinent questions at one time rather than sending them off on the dreaded "run-around," and cut through red tape with a machete in order to help the student achieve his or her goals. Even if all staff members are generally aware of the needs and problems of adult learners, the outreach effort will flounder without a person at the front door who has a coordinating and advocacy role.

One person needs to keep track of ongoing community contacts, monitor data gathering efforts, serve as spokesperson for nontraditional student programs, and build ongoing support within the college. It does not matter whether the coordinator is in Student Services, Academic Affairs or Continuing Education, so long as he or she is well qualified and has adequate clerical and monetary support and ongoing affirmation by supervisors.

The coordinator should try to involve as many faculty members and students in outreach efforts and program development and therefore must possess considerable administrative and human relations skills, as well as a zest for learning and an innovative approach to problems.

Another important function for a coordinator involves protecting the outreach program or special office from political attacks and budget cuts. When competition for shrinking resources threatens the program, the coordinator needs to be ready to defend it with facts, figures, alliances, and advocates. The computer may already contain information needed to justify the program's existence—*if* it is asked to show the number of students over twenty-five, which ones took outreach courses for the first time, and how many subsequent courses were taken and credits generated.

Training for college personnel who deal with adult learners should be instituted. This includes the entire hierarchy from clerical people through the department heads and chief administrators. Those who believe that adult learners do not need special treatment are the ones who never think to explain the CLEP exams or who don't know about drop-in child care services. The nontraditional students themselves are best qualified to enlighten the staff about problems and barriers. In role play situations, they can ask the coordinator of the summer session why the only social activities provided are "keggers" and sock hops when adults living in the dorms (they *do* live in dorms at times) have petitioned for their fees to be spent on tutoring, study skills, and pot luck dinners with faculty members. They can ask the chair of the academic affairs committee why the college will grant thirty credits for a university year for action assignment on an Indian reservation, but not allow credit for prior learning during a year spent doing social work in Harlem.

Training sessions should include not only coverage of the characteristics of diverse adult learners, current services and needs, policy issues, and outreach efforts, but also a request that they assist in the recruitment effort by personally talking about it to their friends, and by adapting their behavior to their new insights. Large and small changes may be equally important in making adults feel welcome, from creating individualized degree programs to staying open during the lunch hour and after 5 P.M., to providing toys in the office (nontraditional students frequently are parents).

The admission process should be simplified and adapted to adult realities. Admission forms should be shortened, or adults told that they need not fill out parts requesting their parents' names or major intentions if they are undecided. They should be reassured that taking one course is as acceptable as taking five. Prohibitive matriculation and transcript fees should be eliminated, especially for "special" students who only want to take one or two courses.

Most adult students need thorough explanations of such things as credits, majors, core requirements, audits, drops and adds, deadlines, and registration procedures. Many are too shy to ask. The forms and schedules are likely to be seen as complicated documents, replete with codes and abbreviations which are indecipherable. Initial academic advising should include a "walk through" of the registration process done over and over until the student shows that he or she can do it alone. Care should be taken to elicit concerns and questions, even when the adult looks self-assured.

Entry level advising should entail a checklist of essential information that the adult needs to know in order to make use of the college's resources. The advisor should discuss the student's general and specific goals, clearly explain the options available, outline the benefits and services that are conferred by student status (especially things like low cost health care for the student, the spouse and the children, discount prices on performing arts and sports events, career advising, counseling, and student organizations), explain the role of a faculty advisor, summarize special options like credit for prior learning and independent study (unheard-of for most adults), and clarify ways to solve problems if they arise (like substituting one course for another, refund policies, grievance procedures, how to get tutoring, and so on).

Providing this kind of information in writing may be helpful, but it is more effective to explain things face to face and answer the individual's questions, using the written material as back-up. Most adults need to be shown how a catalogue and course schedule are used. If they understand, they will not be calling your office with questions!

Try the "buddy system" for helping students get through registration. Many experienced adult learners are more than willing to be a "buddy" to new students. On many campuses they have organized themselves to not only team up with incoming adults, escort them through registration and help them plan their schedule, but also arrange for child care, car pools, and family suppers which help the spouses to get involved in the college.

Services and Programs for Adults

It is obvious that if adult learners do not feel that the college has anything valuable to offer them, they will not take advantage of it. While traditional degree programs and student activities may meet the needs of some, they may not make use of them unless bridges are built. New services will also need to be instituted. These may include: individualized degree programs; credit for prior learning; wider use of the College Level Examination Program (CLEP); more varieties of "testing out of" or "challenging" regular courses; developmental courses aimed at enhancing reading, writing and math skills; study skills and tutoring services; a nontraditional student club or network; a lounge and office for nontraditional students; a newsletter or place in the college newspaper for events of interest; high quality, low cost child care services; hiring adult students to recruit others, provide orientation and advising, or consult with various offices about becoming more responsive to adult needs; counselors who will run support groups and counsel adults in transition;

career "fairs" and workshops designed with adults in mind; graduate student interns assigned to work directly with adult students as counselors, group leaders, activities organizers, and so on; a college-wide advisory committee to continue improving services to adults; special recognition for outstanding work on behalf of students, staff, and faculty to foster lifelong learning.

In summary, colleges wanting to increase access for lifelong learners must decide to do a number of things:

1. Agree to do whatever is necessary to create educational options based on the *student's* needs. This may entail a willingness to alter the degree granting process to allow for credit for past experience, interdisciplinary studies, on the job internships, or a ten year program of part time study;

2. Insist upon quality and integrity of degree requirements, based on institutional standards, but acknowledge the validity of different modes of learning and instruction in meeting those standards;

3. Support proactive and innovative outreach projects which bring the college out into the community;

4. Assign responsibility and provide institutional resources to an individual and staff for recruiting adult students, and serving their needs as they proceed into and through the college;

5. Recognize the importance of person to person communication in recruiting adults, and the importance of promoting feelings of self-confidence and belongingness in lifelong learners;

6. Involve the entire college or university staff in recognizing the needs of diverse adults, adapting programs and services, and joining in the recruitment effort. The consistent message from the trustees and president on down to the receptionists should be "we're glad you're here, and we'll do what we can to be of service to you."

One definition of the word "recruit" is "to furnish or replenish with a fresh supply; renew; restore health or strength." Colleges that have taken systematic steps to respond effectively to the learning needs of diverse adults have reaped benefits beyond the increased FTE count. Adult learners bring fresh ideas into the classroom. Faculty develop new and better modes of teaching which benefit all students. The system becomes more flexible, and the new learners bring strength and health to the institution by sharing their life experiences.

References

Cross, K. P. "New Students of the 70s." *Research Reporter,* 1971, *6* (4), 1–5.

Weathersby, G. "The New Learners." In A. W. Chickering and others (Eds.), *Developing the College Curriculum.* Washington, D.C.: Council for the Advancement of Small Colleges, 1977.

Linda Reisser is dean for students at Whatcom Community College in Bellingham, Washington.

A look at some of the factors that question whether the traditional methods of "dispensing" higher education offer the best formats for learning.

Options for Lifelong Learners: The External Degree

Gordon Cowperthwaite

Two year colleges need to decide the road they will travel into their future, whether they will ask students to adapt to their way of life — a nice but limited luxury perhaps — or whether they will overrule caution and begin to provide the flexibility needed in adapting to a revolution in adult learning, and the content to fulfill individual and social needs. In terms of adult learners, the risk is exacerbated when lockstep processes are imposed upon self-directed and highly motivated people. In fact, the student withdrawal lists are indicators of how traditional programs and traditional delivery systems can fail the needs and expectations of adult learners who often are looking for re-education, or are late bloomers suddenly realizing the importance of education (or its joy), but find that the system is not interested in them except on its own terms. In our throwaway society with its concomitant acceptance of impermanence, it has taken quite a while for such a waste of a "natural" resource to create a ripple on the pool of conscience.

After all, a large number of adult learners are interested in developing abilities which generally are clearly defined and have a pragmatic focus: how can they do something that they know they want to do, like improve job skills, prepare for a career change, learn a new vocational skill, "improve myself." But what is offered must be relevant to their lives as they see it, not because an institution says it is. This is a direct challenge to programs of study as well as to ways in which they are dispensed. Traditionally the criteria espoused for college learning were narrow, based in part on the nineteenth-century model of a society with a trained elite. Exemplary alternative degree programs at Community College of Vermont, Everette College, Whatcom Community College, William Rainey Harper College, Inver Hills Community College, Bunker Hill Community College, and Sinclair Community College are confronting this elitist legacy and are pointing the finger of suspicion at those who maintain that the distribution of higher education of the masses in nontraditional ways will mean the abrogation of "academic standards." But more of this later.

Higher education is moving in a new direction, one which embraces student diversity. Although most educators are aware of the harbinger of student demographics, it would be unfair to say that shifting from a posture of educating the elite to educating the masses is solely the result of competitive pressures and shrinking accounts receivable. Sensitive antennae in colleges and universities all over the country have picked up signals from a widening spectrum of lifelong learners seeking opportunities to grow. But they are seeking such opportunities in a variety of ways which are compatible with their lifestyles and learning styles. They are seeking avenues which will clearly support their goals and aspirations; and for many it is an education less abstract and more experiential.

New Options for Teachers

As this new student group demands an increasing voice in the choice of what colleges offer, we see a wider range of learning alternatives being created, although not yet in a wide array of institutions. Such a stirring up of tradition creates a turbulance felt throughout the campuses but it is not all negative. New options for learning can create new relationships between the faculty and the students that provide faculty members with good opportunities for personal and professional growth. In some alternative degree programs, working with individual differences and applying knowledge about stages of adult development and the adult life cycle can create a mentor-student partnership with immeasurably satisfying consequences for each.

To act upon individual differences in terms of student development becomes the challenge which leads to new roles for us as teachers, new insight into our own strengths and weaknesses, and new opportunities for effective service.

Chickering's work at Empire State College involving adult development (ego development, intellectual development, and ethical development) and the life cycle points the way toward a clearer view of how students learn, both in terms of student self-understanding and faculty appreciation of different learning styles. Chickering asks the question: "can we increase our capacity to recognize and act on individual differences more effectively—both as an institution in terms of developing alternatives and resources and as individual mentors and administrators in terms of working directly with students?" He answers (1976, p. 5): "I think we can. Research and theory concerning the major areas and stages of adult development is a good place to start. This approach is useful because (1) it identifies significant areas of individual differences; (2) it describes major dimensions of learning and development important to college students; and (3) it has powerful implications for students' educational motives, orientations toward knowledge, teaching practices, approaches to evaluation, and student-faculty relationships."

A New Look at Elders

The graying of America is the graying of the campus, too. The Mondale Bill on lifelong learning passed in 1975 makes mandatory the assessment of the educational needs of older and retired persons. The Age Discrimination Act which became effective in January of this year will have significant impact on campuses everywhere. Even a quick look at the statistics on aging shows the huge growth which can be expected in this older group during the next twenty-five years. As people retire earlier, those at fifty-five or even fifty will face problems of time and leisure now faced by people sixty and sixty-five, especially as technological advances in medicine help this group to stay healthier longer. Growing old will remain an active stage of living, not a passive one.

What can community colleges do to demonstrate interest in those persons fifty-five and older who make up a large and currently increasing segment of the population? First of all, they can come up with imaginative opportunities to meet the real needs of this group which frequently include flexible time and location criteria for learning. New programs will have to move beyond the general current practice of opening the campus to "golden agers," which usually means the use of the library, the volleyball courts (or more sedentary activities) and enrolling in traditional courses for "enrichment."

The agism syndrome in this country has created a constellation of prejudices and opinions concerning elders (those persons sixty years and older). Agism tends to create and reinforce false stereotypes about certain modes of behavior which are considered "correct" for them, such as the fact that elders can't learn; are interested only in entertainment and are therefore to be set aside to forage for the remnants of their lives like old cattle fenced off from the herd. On the contrary, most elders are perfectly able (many times eager) to meet rigorous intellectual demands and need to be offered classes and courses which involve psychological, personal, and occupational needs related to their stage of the life cycle. Allen Tough's studies of adult learning (1978) indicate the extent to which adults of all ages are engaged in self-directed learning activities. Reducing or eliminating fees is fine, but there is more to meeting our obligation to these special people than that. Inviting elders to eat in the cafeteria, use the learning resources center, the physical activity facilities, and attend classes free is not sufficient commitment to satisfy our collective conscience. Other areas of concern include pensions, social security, investments, legal services (wills, frauds, obtaining rights), physical fitness programs, information on aging itself (death and dying), crisis management, nursing care, and so on. In addition, for those "younger" elders who are facing the closing out of a productive working life, there is great need for retirement programs in order to tackle such related problems as lack of role definition, retirement shock, retirement and housing, retirement and spouse, and retirement health and nutrition, to mention just a few of the more pressing ones. It is not inconceivable that many of these programs will have to become a part of the institution's "road show" as the idea of the "community as campus" beckons a responsiveness which is less tradition bound and more ecumenical.

Crediting Prior Experiential Learning

Some community colleges, affirming the existence of college level learning resulting from prior experience, have developed delivery systems to provide lifelong learners with opportunities to demonstrate competencies which may lead to credit and credentials. Assessing prior experiential learning is not new, but few colleges provide a comprehensive and flexible system. At Sinclair, any student may enroll in Portfolio Development and portfolio faculty work with students across all disciplines of the college and in several locations, as courses are scheduled to suit the needs of the students, both on the main campus and at neighborhood centers. Portfolio classes begin as group sessions and then become individualized as students arrange appointments with faculty when they find it necessary to discuss particular problems related to development and documentation. The entire prior learning portfolio program is tied into the credit system at the College. Students receive credit for the portfolio development course and additional credit when evaluating faculty agree that previous learning meets instructional requirements.

Reaching Beyond the Campus

Another outreach opportunity for community college portfolio developers is to conduct prior learning portfolio classes at businesses and agencies around the city. Sinclair works with employees at private and public agencies such as Inland, Wright Patterson Air Force Base, and United Way, to help them identify prior learning at the college level. This learning is described and documented through the development of a portfolio which, like the portfolio process described previously, may lead to the granting of course credit. Such programs take the campus to the community in order to make this aid to lifelong learning as convenient as possible for adult students. Again, the goal is to provide time and space for students who might otherwise not be able to conform to rigid time and class schedules required for on-campus learning.

A further way to cement relationships between academic and business, industry, and service communities—which again reflects the idea of time and space flexibility—is to provide specially designed education relevant to those needs and to the times in which we live, such as experiences planned at different times and in different places on site: the off-campus campus. In order to determine the need, faculty can be given release time to make contacts with community practitioners concerning their special requirements and to develop other off-campus activities. Programs like this tend to strengthen relationships between campus and community and provide the teachers involved with a pool of resource people whom they may be able to use as guest lecturers and whom the college may be able to recruit as adjunct faculty. Such a program is in the formative stages between Sinclair and Monsanto Chemical in Miamisburg, Ohio. The success of this kind of program depends on educational institutions realizing that it is academically ethical and economically prudent to their long-term interest to serve the special needs of the broader community by encouraging flexibility in program design and service.

Learning Contracts for Lifelong Learners

A comment by William Glasser in *Schools Without Failure* expresses a concern which clearly leads to a rationale for a program of individualized study and its nontraditional appeal to adult learners: "Today much of what we call education is merely knowledge gathering and remembering. Problem solving, and thinking, never strong parts of our educational system, have been downgraded. . . . At all levels of education we have now an intense effort, perhaps reaching its peak in college and graduate school, to program people with predictable knowledge in the same way our computers are programmed. . . . Education emphasizes a lesser function of the human brain, memory, while relatively neglecting its major function, thinking" (1969, p. 35).

If community college programs are to attract an increasing body of lifelong learners, they must be concerned with experiential learning, with personalizing education, with loosening external controls, with flexible time and place requirements, with proactive learning, with affective development of the students, and with furthering the development of a host of other lifelong learning skills involving career research and counseling, values clarification, coping with change, and other relevant topics. It is very important for these programs to encourage a balance of cognitive and affective development to promote confluent learning with more assurance than the traditional approach with its heavy emphasis upon memorization and feedback, lockstep group activity, and little or marginal student teacher interaction.

In many external degree programs the learning contract is the pivot upon which the idea of individualization turns. Learning contracts allow the student to influence the learning to a great degree. Ideally this influence will reflect the student's learning style so that he or she can capitalize on modes of study most productive to lasting knowledge. Some students learn best through avid reading, research, and writing; others find learning more meaningful when it is largely experiential, where reading is balanced with interaction with human resources in and beyond the college. The best learning contracts are those which provide options and are designed to capitalize on the strengths and minimize the weaknesses of its creators. In many programs of this kind learning takes place through the vehicle of a contract involving the student, a faculty facilitator (sometimes called a core faculty), and perhaps several teaching faculty (sometimes called mentors) who approve the contract and make final evaluation for grades and credit. Core faculty work independently but closely with the student to assist him or her in developing contract components, to assume a student advocacy role with mentors, and to provide multidimensional support aimed at successful student growth. Learning contracts normally focus on three areas: (1) objectives or competencies to be mastered, (2) learning activities keyed to that mastery, and (3) evaluation of the products of the learning activities to make sure learning has taken place in terms of the course objectives.

A learning contract might best be envisioned by comparing it to a classroom experience. In a typical classroom setting for a course in marketing management, students listen to lectures, read assigned chapters in a text, may explore some additional resources such as the *Journal of Marketing,* take tests, and perhaps complete a project. But all of this is done in a prescribed time frame such as a quarter or a semester, and learning is not self-paced, but lock-step.

A learning contract is an individualizing experience and, depending upon the scope of the project, time-flexible. The marketing student may or may not read the textbook, but may opt to explore parts of several recommended texts, delve into periodic literature with a focus on certain industry-related marketing problems, interview two or three marketing managers to find out the key issues in current marketing practice (such as the effect of rapidly rising gasoline prices on distribution cost effectiveness), do a contrast paper on the marketing strategies of three different kinds of goods retailers, or arrange for an internship in the marketing department of a local manufacturer. These learning activities, articulated clearly in the contract, and related to course objectives, lead into a variety of products for evaluation reflecting the reading, the interview experiences, the internship and the rich body of experiential learning which has resulted from a panorama of resources. There is increasing evidence (Tough, 1978) to suggest that such intense and highly self-directing activity produces learning which is deeper and more permanent than that which is "taught." K. Patricia Cross talks about the distinction between adult education and adult learning, defining adult education as being concerned with providing instruction for adults, whereas adult learning emphasizes the facilitating of learning:

Following this distinction, the supporters of adult education are defined as those who work toward equal opportunity and the improved access for adults. . . . Their emphasis would be on getting adults into an educational system (offered by industry, churches, and community agencies as well as by schools and colleges) that mainly provides group instruction on either a credit or noncredit basis.

The advocates of adult learning, on the other hand, would bend their efforts toward facilitating individual learning on any topic of interest to the learner, through providing mentors, learning contracts and learning exchanges, counseling and advisory systems, and the like. They would give relatively little attention to providing access to instruction and certification and relatively more attention to helping people plan their own learning programs (1978, p. 1).

Programs at Community College of Vermont and Sinclair Community College offer alternatives to "instruction," placing the learner central to the institutional process by offering contract learning which allows considerable student influence over learning activity, thus "facilitating individual learning" as contrasted to group learning in fixed time boundaries. Bloom's theories of mastery learning have relevance to this form of learning activity. The self-pacing nature of most contract learning supports individual differences and does allow for the time factor to play its part in mastering competencies. In addition to the cognitive improvement possible through self-paced learning, the possible improved self-concept as a result of success (the affective area) made possible by self-imposed time frames may be the most important contri-bution to furthering a love of learning which can last a lifetime.

Cross reports that one of the most important findings from the various studies of adult self-planned learning is that adults simply want to have more control over the learning process and, therefore, choose self-directed study over formal classroom instruction. The Penland (1977) study confirms what many educators are now beginning to take seriously: the adult learners want to use their own learning style in a format which provides for self-pacing.

Two Examples of Contract Learning

At Community College of Vermont students are offered an associate degree in which they develop individualized study plans, or contracts, focus-ing on their areas of competence. Each student works with a trained instruc-tor-counselor who helps him or her to assess what each has learned and wants to learn. Jointly the student and instructor plan ways to reach learning goals, implement the plans, and evaluate the new learning. A local review committee composed of the student, a community practitioner, a teacher, and a College staff member works closely with the student and counselor to guide and to val-

64

idate the learning contract. Such CCV programs identify certain competencies which have to be mastered, but they do not specify how they should be learned. This provides students with a wide spectrum of choice in creating their own curriculum. Learning from prior experience, present employment, academic courses, independent study, or volunteer service may be used to focus on degree requirements. Narrative evaluations are provided and the degree is awarded when the student has demonstrated mastery of the skills and knowledge defined in the study plan. At Community College of Vermont there is no time limit set for degree completion as the program is self-pacing and is designed to fit the student's learning style.

At Sinclair Community College the College Without Walls program is offered to students in management, marketing, mid-management retailing, labor studies, psychology, sociology, early childhood education, and fine and commercial art. Seven core faculty work with thirty faculty mentors (teaching faculty evaluators) to assist students in planning and implementing learning activities and in designing forms of evaluation. At Sinclair Community College, competencies already are defined by the College, so students have input at only two levels of the contract: learning activities and evaluation.

Under the Sinclair College Without Walls program it is intended that learning must be a dynamic process, a process where students are invested with the major responsibility for learning. Students are offered these basic parameters:

1. A fluid concept of time which allows for self-pacing and the possibility for broader and deeper learning.
2. A variety of potential locations for learning such as in the home, on the job, in the community, in service to others, or in other educational and learning resource locations.
3. A variety of evaluation possibilities including on-site evaluation, reflection papers, simulations, role playing, as well as the College's newly developed evaluation of prior learning process.
4. A breadth of resources beyond the College, including expert opinions of community practitioners, area university and college instruction, city-wide learning resources, field experiences, traditional tests and reading, audiovisual materials and modules available through the Dayton/Miami Valley Consortium of Colleges and Universities.

For further exposition of contract learning, read Susan Mancuso's article, "The Community as the Classroom—Contract Learning in the Community," in the Summer 1979 issue of CAEL Community College Newsletter.

What Does It Mean for the Future?

Ronald Gross (1976, p. 15) believes "the alternatives movement in higher education endeavors to provide other options. It seeks to facilitate higher learning for people of all ages and conditions of life, relevant to their highly individual goals and aspirations and according to their requirements and constraints."

Ernest L. Boyer (1972, p. 8) discusses the problems of nineteenth-century models of education reflecting a society which no longer exists: "This model of the self-contained campus—well-rooted in the circumstances of the time—has been locked into an iron vise of custom and still forms our image of the way 'things ought to be.' And while our world has been transformed around us, we still cling to a mental picture of higher education that would have been entirely familiar to our great-great-grandparents. We are, in short, in one of those periods of lag, in which an institution evolves more slowly than the society it serves."

There is no question that millions of Americans are seeking new educational "products" which mirror the changes taking place in our society and which are embedded more in reality than in the wispy nostalgia for the old academy. However, it's not a question of the good guys versus the bad guys, the traditionalists versus the futurists, the classroom versus the external degree, but the imperative to examine the *process,* not the setting as the sine qua non of educational relevance.

New approaches to learning often are a threat to established practices because initially, at any rate, they are beyond our power to press into familiar molds. The question facing community colleges today is not so much the conforming process, but the breaking of the molds themselves. Boyer continues: "The point is that for increasing numbers of college age young people—as well as for countless thousands of adults—the external degree approach offers the alternatives they have been seeking, and that, rather than proliferating endlessly the campus model, we should create flexible alternatives to match the need."

What About Quality Assurance?

The issue of quality assurance always lurks below the surface of any discussion of nontraditional approaches to learning. External degree programs absorb their share of flak from the guns of tradition and their case certainly has not been helped by the unconscionable fly-by-nights who have perpetrated their fraud upon the trusting. I mentioned earlier the fear of the abrogation of academic standards. It is not so much the threat to "standards" which new programs present—unless the word "standards" is defined as clearly predetermined curricula for eighteen- to twenty-one-year-olds who live on campus and follow historically determined programs—but the opening of options to provide relevant, individualized education for students of all ages and conditions of life.

Tight standards of achievement can prevail with the new egalitarianism so long as the monitoring of the work is done by teachers who prize the diversity which individual differences produce and who will measure each student's performance in terms of the progress being made toward stated learning outcomes as they would with any other student.

So flexibility in program and delivery is not automatically one side of the equation of failure. Such programs must provide for quality assurance, of course, and from our experience with the College Without Walls program at Sinclair Community College we know that it is possible to provide flexible programs of directed independent study with exemplary student performance in a very high percentage of the cases.

Boyer puts it rather well when he says (1972, p. 8): "It seems to me that the 'quality' of an individual's education depends upon four fundamental conditions: (1) A student with a motivation to learn; (2) Teachers to channel that motivation toward clear educational objectives; (3) The availability of resources adequate to achieve those objectives; and (4) Rigorous evaluation of both the students and the institution to determine how well those objectives are being achieved." He concludes the article with the following statement (p. 8): "The individual campus is coming to seem less like a fortress surrounded by its moat, and more like a supermarket of ideas, a library with easy access, or a base of operations to coordinate learning, not control it."

One may add an "amen!" to this because it is clearly important to realize that the exciting variety of nontraditional opportunities available for lifelong learners are important pathways to knowledge and self-fulfillment, not trolls under the bridge of the traditional educational process.

References

Boyer, E. L. "We Must Find New Forms of Higher Education." *The Chronicle of Higher Education,* 1972, *6* (19), 8.

Chickering, A. W. *A Conceptual Framework for Educational Alternatives at Empire State College.* Saratoga Springs, N.Y.: Empire State College, 1976.

Cross, K. P. "The Adult Learner." In K. P. Cross and others, (Eds.), *The Adult Learner. Current Issues in Higher Education, 1978.* Washington, D.C.: American Association for Higher Education, 1978.

Glasser, W. *Schools Without Failure.* New York: Harper & Row, 1969.

Gross, R. *Diversity in Higher Education: Reform in the Colleges.* Bloomington, Ind.: Phi Delta Kappa Educational Foundation, Fastback 69, 1976.

Mancuso, S. "The Community as the Classroom—Contract Learning in the Community." *CCN-CAEL Newsletter,* Community College Network of the Council for Advancement of Experiential Learning, Issue Four, Summer 1979.

Penland, P. R. *Individual Self-Planned Learning in America.* Washington, D.C.: Department of Health, Education, and Welfare, 1977.

Tough, A. "Major Learning Efforts: Recent Research and Future Directions." In K. P. Cross and others, (Eds.), *The Adult Learner. Current Issues in Higher Education, 1978.* Washington, D.C.: American Association for Higher Education, 1978.

67

Watkins, B. T. "Easing the Trauma of Going Back to College." *The Chronicle of Higher Education,* 1978, *16* (20), 3.

Gordon Cowperthwaite is a core faculty person with the College Without Walls program at Sinclair Community College.

*State and federal laws and administrative regulations, funding
formulas, and cooperative policies for colleges, communities,
business, and industry must be revised in order to advance
lifelong learning.*

Lifelong Education:
The Critical Policy Questions

Jamison Gilder

Community colleges are one of the nation's best resources for serving lifelong
learners. They are convenient, flexible, responsive, widespread institutions
with a successful history of services to adults. More than any other postsecondary institutions, community colleges are adapting to change. Their programs,
schedules, services, and facilities have been evolving along with their students.
They have, in fact, been the primary access to postschool learning for many
groups of people, and they have done a very good job of helping them.

     Our policy framework is one important area where we still need to
catch up with the times. The policy framework includes funding legislation,
board regulations, accreditation guidelines, financial aid rules, new program
development procedures, and other "guidelines" we use in decision making.
Many operational policies for community colleges were legislated, however,
when new community colleges opened at the rate of one a week. And twenty-
year-old policies don't suit today's students or today's colleges.

     Many of the now common programs and services for lifelong learners
appeared in spite of a restrictive policy framework. Evening and weekend
courses, television courses, daycare services, credit for prior learning, and
cooperative programs with employers are examples of community college
developments that serve lifelong learners despite the aging policy structure.
They are being reviewed for needed change and development in a three year

"Policies for Lifelong Education" effort by the American Association of Community and Junior Colleges.

One activity of the Policies for Lifelong Education project was to convene a national assembly. The assembly developed a series of forty-five action recommendations to advance lifelong education. It also adopted the following statement on the needs for learning (Gilder, 1979, 111–112):

> Lifelong education is moving from theory to fact for increasing numbers of persons in our society. The growing complexities of earning a living and being a competent participant in the community are making this development a necessity. It is no longer feasible to plan on a period of education that extends only through the late teens or early twenties to carry us through life in the latter part of the Twentieth Century. If our lives are to be fulfilling, if our communities are to be livable, if our industry is to be productive, if our society is to be healthy, we must have the opportunity for education throughout our lives.
>
> Our educational system has developed many instruments to meet this need: schools, colleges, churches, libraries, museums, businesses, unions, the Armed Forces, and other agencies have developed responsible educational services. Education in the arts and sciences, education for occupations and for leisure, are becoming available to more persons, in more places, and at more times. Useful patterns of cooperation among providers of these services have developed in many instances.
>
> The policy framework, however, has not kept up with the developing needs and the variety of responses. Laws, regulations, guidelines, directives, funding formulas, and other elements that make up the policy framework need to be brought up to date—along with the data and attitudes out of which such policies are developed. The changing demography and lifestyle of our society must be recognized in educational policies and practices. Assessments of educational needs, cooperation among agencies must be facilitated, not frustrated, by the policies of public or private agencies.
>
> We believe the leadership for needed changes should be initiated at local levels through assessments of local needs for lifelong education made cooperatively by the institutions and citizens concerned. The support of public and private agencies and of local, state, and federal governments should be sought through unified action based on well-documented needs and priorities.

Recommendations of the Assembly were arranged by target groups and were directed to individual colleges; AACJC; local, county, state, and federal governments; and the private sector. Full text of the Assembly report and its background issue papers are published elsewhere. This paper comments on the content and categories of action needed rather than the target groups named earlier.

Seven basic categories of effort emerged to encourage and support life-long education:

1. A call for strong support statements—widely adopted and distributed—that lifelong education is a basic human right and a national capital asset. Community colleges and other lifelong education providers need to be clearly recognized for the nature and strength of their support for adult learning opportunities.

2. Fundamental change in both the mission and structure of adult-centered institutions. Analysis and development of enabling legislation, governance, and operations policies will be needed. These may involve changes in administration, scheduling, credit awards, financial aid, faculty composition, facilities, and contracts for cooperation.

3. Expansion of collaborative linkages with other providers. This cooperation and linkage can occur at several levels (local, state, or federal), but it may be most important at the local level. Without the give and take that makes new resources available and expands opportunity to more learners, fundamental institutional change will be little noticed. Trustees will play a crucial new leadership role in establishing these linkages and collaborative relationships with their neighbors in the community.

4. Improving local assessments of adult learners' needs. Public hearings were suggested repeatedly. Other techniques include community forums, outreach mailing research, direct neighborhood contacts, and interviews with students. Program priorities and activities should better reflect the findings of local assessment.

5. Adjustments in the funding mechanisms which support lifelong education. Expanded or refitted funding formulas—as well as entirely new financing patterns—will be needed to serve both the new clientele and the "new" institutions. State legislative general fund appropriations driven by old FTE- or ADA-based formulas need to be adjusted. Good cost benefit research will be needed to establish less restrictive funding mechanisms.

6. More recognition and acceptance of the increasing role of labor, business, and industry in lifelong education. Most adult lives are job centered, and the employer provides life enrichment opportunities as well as a living. Searching discussions are needed to understand which providers play which roles in adult learning and development.

7. Continuous affirmation that full equity and equal access are central goals of lifelong education. One standard to measure our progress is the extent to which we can "empower our consumers." This will require a greater understanding of adult learning and processes which enable individuals to know more about themselves—about who they are, what they want, and what their own responses and reactions are. Moreover, we should anticipate these needs in the context of the unusual demographic revolution around us. The popula-

tion will be more aged, there will be a decline in fertility, women learners will increase their numbers, and there will be substantial increases in the number of American minorities. For instance, there will be fifteen to twenty million Mexican-Americans—with adult learning needs and equity rights. We can already begin to plan for such needs.

Vigorous activity in each of these seven areas is underway at AACJC and by many members of the Assembly. Since this volume is entitled *Serving Adult Learners,* I will concentrate here on efforts and recommendations aimed most directly at learner services, commenting on the seven categories above.

Support Statements

The Assembly recommended "that strong support be given to the current national policy stated in Title I-B, Section 131 (8) of the Higher Education Act which states: 'American society should have as a goal the availability of appropriate opportunities for lifelong learning for all its citizens without regard to restrictions of previous education or training, sex, age, handicapping conditions, social or ethnic background, or economic circumstances.' " It also asked "that support be given to the concept of lifelong education as a means for all citizens to develop competencies which will enable them to live productive and satisfying lives."

Also, a Bill of Rights for the Lifelong Learner eloquently described ideal opportunities to enrich our lives:
1. Every adult American has the right to continue to learn throughout life;
2. Every adult American has the right to equal opportunity for access to relevant learning opportunities at each stage of life;
3. Diversity and access to education opportunity are important to democracy in the United States;
4. Any index of the quality of life in the United States includes opportunities for growth and self-actualization as a right of the learning society;
5. Neither age, nor sex, nor creed, nor ethnic background, nor marital status, nor disability should create barriers to the opportunity to continue to grow through participation in organized learning activities;
6. Coping, living, working are dimensions which exemplify the range of learning needs of the learning society;
7. Public investment in the learning society is an investment in human capital and in the human condition.

Mission and Structural Changes

Community colleges are very conveniently positioned to deliver needed services at the community level, and lifelong education is becoming one of their primary purposes. The Assembly recommended:

That community colleges make an institution-wide commitment to lifelong education. Institutional policies should reflect this institutional commitment. Policies and practices that are barriers to lifelong education should be revised.

That community colleges collaborate with other community agencies to define the clientele to be served through lifelong education, to shape educational programs to meet consumer needs, and to provide access for all clientele into appropriate programs.

That community colleges seek private and public funding to enhance the professional development of counselors, faculty members, and administrators so all staff may better meet the needs of the adult learner.

That faculty members be aware of the roles they play in regard to lifelong education and receive special training in working with adult learners.

There is a growing consensus that lifelong learning is an accepted and appropriate activity in our society. Community colleges appear to be the "logical conduit" for lifelong learning: There are 1240 community colleges in the country, and they are located in *426 out of 435 congressional districts.* There were four million credit students as of the opening fall enrollment in 1977. Their average age is twenty-seven years old, and there are over 3,500,000 people involved in other community service programs in these institutions.

Citizen interest in receiving services and institutional responses have grown so fast that, to some extent, public support, institutional capabilities, and professional know-how have been outpaced. Management and staff, in many situations, are learning how to provide new services, in new locations, under new arrangements, as they go along. Successful models and experiences need to be shared and disseminated.

The Association itself is also changing and expanding. At its annual meeting in 1979, the Board approved the expansion of membership eligibility to regionally accredited proprietary schools. This brings the services and programs of the national association to thousands more learners than in previous years.

Plans are underway to follow up the national assembly with a series of four state assemblies during 1980 and 1981. These assemblies will develop further recommendations — more specific and detailed — indigenous to the particular state given its history of traditions and services. Sites will be selected for the regional assemblies that offer promise for practical review of problems and recommended solutions as well as guideline practices to be encouraged.

Preparations for change are also occurring at the state leadership level. Governor James B. Hunt, Jr. of North Carolina wrote the opening statement for the national assembly. He also sent its report and recommendations to the other forty-nine governors with a letter calling on them to establish specific task forces to enhance lifelong education opportunity.

To expand the planning for change, AACJC will initiate a large national series of community discussions (using forums, hearings, and other techniques) in the fall of 1980. This process will contribute to wider citizen involvement in determining the future mission of the community college and services to lifelong learners.

Expanded Collaborative Linkages

Sharper definitions of functions—along with a clearer picture of the total task and possible strategies—are needed to increase cooperation and to expand community linkage. The Policies for Lifelong Education Assembly recommended:

> That the AACJC give top priority to giving leadership to its member institutions in order that they may become institutions for life-long education. The member institutions should be encouraged to cooperate with other institutions and agencies in their communities in the development and delivery of lifelong education services.
>
> That college presidents take the initiative in bringing together community representatives from all organizations and institutions which provide lifelong education experiences and that the various groups join together to sponsor a community educational information center.
>
> That community college trustees familiarize themselves with local needs for lifelong education and provide local leadership in the development of policies to facilitate lifelong learning services. Trustees should also help interpret the services to the community to help build support for them.

Because we have as a nation tried to solve our past problems with big government and with big scale institutions, we do not have smaller associations which can mediate between large institutions and individuals. A very fragile and critical element in American life is emerging—a phenomenon of people associated with one another in neighborhood organizations and in neighborhood identifications. This is not a framework of large scale institutions. It presents the question of how to transfer both the resources and authority to voluntary neighborhood associations so that people can begin working directly with problems that trouble them (rather than more strengthening of large public and private institutions). We need to design programs that empower individuals in local institutions rather than big scale institutions and governments already in place. Unfortunately however, many of these smaller scale institutions require vital technical assistance; they need full-time community organizers, and a permanent organization which can endure the peaks and valleys of daily problem solving. Perhaps there is a role to be played by large scale institutions in providing such technical assistance in a hands-off style. Another role which could be played by the large institutions in order to mediate between institutions and individuals would be to design a new structure which would encourage and harness individual participation in neighborhood improvement for the quality of life. Collaborative linkages described here could provide such a mechanism.

The Policies project also conducted a survey of existing cooperative arrangements at a random sample of community colleges. Findings show that—for 134 colleges included—there are an average 99.6 cooperative activities already developed at these colleges!

Trustees are assuming significant new leadership roles in establishing community linkage. A distinguished panel of trustees at a recent forum called for more trustee involvement in coordination among local agencies and development of cooperative programs ("Lifelong Learning," 1979).

Local Assessment of Learning Needs

Lifelong learners are also residents of a local neighborhood. Students do not travel long distances to take advantage of lifelong education. They attend the community colleges partly because those institutions are close to home. This knowledge will help community colleges to conduct community needs assessments, to understand the local neighborhood, and therefore to target the learning opportunities more precisely to the needs of the students. The Assembly recommended:

> That the AACJC make every effort to communicate openly and directly with the learners and solicit their recommendations as policies and procedures on lifelong education are developed.

> That community colleges join with other community organizations to sponsor local assessments and other activities that will result in a current picture of unmet lifelong educational needs. Implicit in this recommendation is the belief that community colleges can work with other organizations to solve social problems. Moreover, community colleges should develop programs which respond to the identified needs of specific segments of the population, such as the economically and educationally disadvantaged, minorities, women, older persons, and physically handicapped.

> That community colleges cooperate with other community agencies to conduct hearings on lifelong education and how to best meet identified needs. Recommendations should be made known to the appropriate community and political leaders.

> That educational agencies reexamine their mission and service priorities in light of changes in society in order to better provide for the needs of new clientele such as older and part-time students. These

agencies should cooperate in conducting comprehensive community needs assessments.

That all agencies, institutions and individuals concerned with the delivery of lifelong education keep in mind the needs of the educational consumer and that the consumer of educational services be consulted regularly regarding programs of lifelong education. Consultation should take place prior to the development of courses, programs, or other activities which will influence the lifelong education of the individual.

Successful local needs assessments can help adult learners overcome barriers to their continued academic, personal, and career development. The characteristics of adult students tell us that the adult part-time students are the largest growing sector of the educational system. They are placing new demands on existing institutions and creating needs for development of new ones. They are encouraging the creation and development of nontraditional programs and approaches to teaching and learning. Although those who already have the most education continue to get more throughout life, we can do more to improve accessibility for nearly all learners.

To prepare for such needs assessments, detailed information on adult enrollment and characteristics of adult learners can be obtained from the NCES data on participation in adult education in 1975. The following data were taken from computer runs from these tapes. (The 1975 data are the latest data available from NCES.) There were 1.5 million students enrolled in adult programs for credit in two year institutions in 1975. Most, in fact 69 percent, were under thirty-four years of age, and 89 percent were white. Sixty percent of the students already had one to three years of college, and 75 percent had over $10,000 of income. Eight out of ten were currently working, and 52 percent were enrolled in courses for high school or college credit. In the matter of payment, there were 64 percent who made payment either by themselves or from their families, 10 percent who were paid for by an employer, and 26 percent who were paid for by public funds. One of the surprising findings which may reflect the five-year change in the nation's value from 1975 to 1980 is that the 1975 participation data show only 1.5 percent (of the students enrolled in two year colleges outlined above) who were enrolled in courses involving "current issues," only 5 percent were involved in personal and family living courses, and only 2 percent in social and recreation courses. This presents a strong contrast to the 52 percent enrolled in general education for credit, the 10 percent enrolled for professional occupational training, and the 20 percent enrolled for technical occupational training.

The 1.5 million students noted above, who were enrolled in a credit course in a two year college in 1975, represent a small fraction of the adults in the country who were participating in adult education. Overall the report shows that 17 million people or 11.6 percent of the over-seventeen-year-old population were participating; 2.1 million of these were enrolled in a credit course in a four year college; 1.5 million, as stated above, were enrolled in a two year college. We can assume that the remainder were enrolled in noncredit courses. The trends since 1975 have continued upward in the area of noncredit enrollment. These may be due to fee changes, restrictions on financial aid, restriction on prior learning conditions, and restrictions on individual confidence in academic work. One of the policy implications in lifelong learning is the credit and noncredit axis. What are the responsibilities for effective social policy to deal with the learning needs of adults whether or not such learning may carry with it the traditionally associated academic credit towards a recognized degree?

In light of these questions, it is fascinating to examine the reasons given by students dropping courses after they were enrolled for credit at two year colleges. The most frequently cited reason for dropping a course was that the course was disappointing or too demanding. The second and third reasons why students dropped courses involved illness of themselves or their family, or an overcrowded personal schedule. These statistics tell us something about how we are not meeting the needs of adult students. We are presenting courses that do not meet their expectations or which are too demanding for their existing skills. We are not providing enough flexibility—with the result that an illness leads to dropping out of a course. And second, we are preventing them from integrating a learning opportunity into the other complexities of their lives, and presenting a course which provides too much to do leads to dropping out.

One of the distinguishing characteristics of adult learners is their involvement in a significant number of other activities besides learning itself. These include marriage, child rearing, work, and community affairs. This can be expected from the characteristics of an adult learner who is usually between the ages of twenty-five and forty, and in at least three out of five cases is a woman. The life circumstances of the adult learner preclude giving 100 percent of their attention to education. They must somehow fit time for their education and learning experiences into a complex situation of many other responsibilities.

For the most part, these adult learners say they are seeking greater self-knowledge and greater self-awareness when they return to institutions. They are interested in learning more about themselves, about life coping skills, and in gaining an understanding of the world in which they operate. The literature in adult development would predict these needs for adult students. The body of research in adult development shows that there is a need to gain greater control of one's life and to realize one's full potential and that there is an increasing drive toward this goal with advancing age. One of the manifestations of this is that we find students trying to fit learning experiences into the complex life patterns described above.

Despite a very strong motivation to return to college in order to learn more about themselves, many of these very students are the ones most under-prepared to face the demands of a new education. They have eighth and ninth grade reading levels and are unable to master the basic computation skills and writing necessary for the learning they seek. There are 57 million people who have not completed high school. One fifth of all adults are functionally illiterate and 15 million of these have less than an eighth grade education. This subpopulation presents very specific problems and policy options in development of lifelong education. They also present the needs for resource sharing, cooperative linkages, and intergroup cooperation.

The institutions are faced, therefore, with a need for a very sensitive intake mechanism for such students and for an ongoing support structure if they are to be encouraged and nurtured. The availability of both counseling and support networks is especially important to adult learners. One other important aspect to provide for such students is an opportunity for career and life planning. Students often prepare portfolios of prior learning in order to obtain credit for experiential learning experiences. It is very important to note that the significance of such a portfolio can be much greater in the learning outcome for an individual student than the token credits which are often received for such a process.

To follow through on the Assembly recommendations, local public hearings are being conducted on the needs for services and programs to serve the lifelong learner. An early set of these hearings at Central Piedmont Community College in Charlotte, North Carolina, was televised by ETIV (the local education TV station) and broadcast live in North Carolina. Also a video cassette synopsis of the hearings will be prepared for sharing with other community colleges undertaking a learner centered, outreach, local needs assessment process. This technique allows any adult citizen to be heard, any need to be expressed, and any program or service to be suggested in a neutral situation. The hearings are one way to provide for participation by nonstudents, place-bound students, and others who might otherwise have restricting limitations.

Adjusting Funding Mechanisms

Translating the concept of lifelong education into legislation and budgetary support is a path with many pitfalls. Maintaining the equity balances while adjusting finance patterns is a delicate process. But to start, our best professionals need to help politicians and policy makers write legislation that assures realistic lifelong education opportunity. Legislation developed in the next few years will help to set educational policy for many people for many years to come. The 1979 Assembly recommended:

> That states change the current patterns of funding based on the generation of full-time equivalent students. The state should consult with the AACJC in their efforts to revise funding formulas.

That the AACJC work cooperatively with the national organizations of mayors, governors, and state legislators to implement policies more favorable to lifelong education.

That states and federal policies eliminate restrictions regarding lifelong education. Among the restrictions which should be examined and perhaps eliminated are prohibitions against unemployment insurance beneficiaries enrolling in educational programs and restrictive welfare policies affecting participation.

That federal legislation be enacted to liberalize allowable deductions and provide personal income tax reductions for education expenditures — credit, noncredit, vocational, and avocational programs.

That such assessments of needs then be translated into statements of priorities that can be used by policy makers. The statements of needs and priorities should be developed in cooperation with interested community organizations. The interested organizations should unite in presenting their statements of needs and priorities to local, state, and federal funding sources, as well as to business, unions, foundations, and other private agencies that can provide support.

In a recent informal survey by Edmund J. Gleazer, Jr., President of the AACJC, 400 community college presidents indicated leading issues concerning them in the next few years: financing, mission clarification, loss of local control, and proliferation of specialized accreditation programs. Because these are such difficult basic issues, considerable discussion and compromise will be needed.

Fiscal allocation and reallocation practices present serious policy problems. This includes not only the need for adjustments regarding who gets which funds — but also creating flexibility to accomodate different situations in different communities. Needs differ. Resources and capabilities differ from community to community. Flexible financial formulas are needed to make possible the fullest utilization of existing resources in a variety of circumstances.

Funding patterns particularly need adjustments to allow and promote the variety of useful cooperative arrangements between learning providers.

Still another problem is the need to demonstrate to taxpayers and legislators that lifelong learning is of economic value and deserves high priority in a time of tight budgets. Measures of learning, productivity, and outcomes that have meaning for the public are needed. Community colleges and other agencies offering lifelong learning must be prepared to report to the public the results of their services in terms that the public can understand and support.

"Part-time students are full-time voters" (Weathersby and Jacobs, 1977). They consider themselves primarily as citizens, taxpayers, voters — not as students — yet they have recurring educational needs. As an aside, it should be noted that while people forty-five and older make up more than half of the electorate, the results of election research show that older Americans vote more regularly than young ones; therefore, the political influence of this group will be out of proportion even to their increasing numbers and will have significant effects on the demands and roles of institutions and programs. And there are between 275 and 400 federal programs which provide support for adult learning opportunities, depending on the definition used for such programs.

In addition to legislative formula change, there are needs to improve tax incentives for individuals who participate as adult learners. The American Society for Training and Development successfully introduced a tax reform package to change the IRS treatment of employer education assistance as taxable employee income. Further changes in the treatment of public assistance and unemployment benefits may also be needed.

Labor, Business, and Industry Roles

The corporate world in America has in the past decade become more socially responsible. There is talk about accountability to employees, to customers, to stock-holders, and to the community. There is also discussion about the share of the corporate world in the support of education, culture, and health.

Development of new jobs, institutional development, and financing development are the future subjects of business, industry, and labor discussions with the higher education community. It is important that these groups understand one another's role in providing education — and where and how they can cooperate with one another. The understanding and support of the business sector and the labor sector will be crucial in changing funding formulas at the state level (in order to support community colleges as they offer learning opportunities to new groups of students).

We know that adults rely on education and training to upgrade and refine their opportunities for a better job and a better life. Policy makers from all sectors can help. By combining career and liberal arts education, we can increase and improve these opportunities by making better use of resources outside of traditional colleges. Education and training is legitimately occurring in many places outside of traditional classrooms.

Sophisticated new technology will make it possible to expand learning and teaching beyond what has ever been imagined. The opportunities are enormous for foundations, for the federal government, for the state, for the major industries, and for the learners themselves to participate in an expansion of learning and sharing. It will, however, be important for these groups to understand the role which each will play in the overall process of expanding this opportunity. New technology is very expensive. Collaborative efforts and sharing resources will be essential if we are to effectively utilize this technology. Without such cooperation, we may lose an opportunity to help develop the economy of our nation and the growth and development of our work force. The assembly on Policies for Lifelong Education recommended:

That the AACJC continue its present relationship with the National Chamber of Commerce and that it work with the Chamber and other national organizations to develop linkages between business and colleges for furthering lifelong education as a means of developing human capital investment in the United States.

That business and industry be asked to contribute to lifelong education needs of workers, especially when such changes as relocation or retooling of an industry take place.

That the development of financing of lifelong education programs be jointly discussed by leaders of industry, labor, and institutions of higher education. These discussions should result in specific proposals that will be mutually supported.

That state and federal agencies strongly support the position that a well-funded lifelong education program is essential to the achievement of our national goals of lowering the rate of inflation, increasing productivity of workers, and decreasing unemployment.

Business, industry, and labor could develop paid educational leave policies, as recommended, to encourage employees to remain up-to-date and active in their job and professional development. Important tools are needed to measure the growth and return of employee sponsored learning to the corporate sector and to measure the contributions of community colleges and other education providers in employee development. Also, specific projects could be undertaken (1) to develop lifelong education modules for sharing with institutions and employers, (2) in changing administrative regulations that sometimes prohibit expansion of learning opportunities in local neighborhoods, and (3) to develop new reimbursement policies for institutions that enroll adult learners and to move away from a FTE/ADA formula to another basis of state funding.

The idea of human capital profit was originally conceived by Merril M. Clark, Senior Vice President for the Academy for Educational Development. Human capital profit can be thought of as a number of talented, trained, and able workers in midcareer and late career who have been produced by our free enterprise system. The challenge is to find ways and means to invest our human capital to promote greater productivity. It is believed that further productivity will help in producing more wealth and wider participation in an economy of abundance. The future health of the corporate sector itself may depend on how well this challenge of investing human capital is met and how much it results in promoting greater productivity.

One of the economic and social questions in the next decade is: How can the surplus of human capital profit be better utilized for the society as a whole? Human capital can be eroded by allowing career crises to lower workers' productivity and through mandatory and premature retirement policies (which rob the economy of human capital). Business, government, and education professionals are concerned that the nation's future may depend heavily on our utilizing human capital profit. If we look at our present condition and our future, we know we must improve employment opportunities for all people including people forty-five and older. This century began with 3 million Americans over age sixty-five; it will end with 30 million; it will increase to 53 million by the year 2030. There is no way we can support that population outside the productive economy. Now is the right time to put our managerial expertise to work on the problem.

There is a central role to be played by the education profession in the solution of this problem, and that is in its ability to offer lifelong learning opportunities to the American work force. The prospect of developing better careers, second careers, and third careers is appealing to many employees, and interest among them in continuing education and also in in-house training programs and retraining programs is growing very rapidly. There is also employee interest in self-appraisal in determining their own abilities and evaluating their performance on the job. Moreover, career planning and life planning can begin at an earlier age than they do now, and can be continued over the lifespan. Part of what individuals require to develop and gain experiences are changes in self-image. They have social, financial, and psychological needs to know more about themselves, their goals, and priorities in order to prepare for a continuing life of productivity.

The seriousness of this problem is also indicated by the attention given by President Carter. He says, "in the next four decades, the number of middle-aged and older citizens will increase more rapidly than ever. We must make a commitment now to guarantee that future generations of older Americans will find meaning and purpose in their middle and latter years through continuing new careers, in employment, through the full exercise of their civic opportunities, through volunteer services in their communities, and through readily available opportunities to pursue their vocational and educational interests."

The United States has a more able older population than any other society has ever produced. There are 65 million people in the country who are over forty-five years of age according to the Bureau of Labor Statistics. Two out of every ten Americans (20 percent of the population) are between forty-five and sixty-five and are active in the work force. By the year 2000, their number will rise to 57 million people, an increase of 36 percent. Another 23 million people, that is, 10 percent, are over sixty-five. They constitute an older, experienced personnel resource. By the next generation, the numbers in each group will likely grow to 30 million people. As a result of our increasing lifespan and our declining birth rate, we can expect that the average age of the American work force is going to advance. Furthermore, this work force will be large, well trained, and experienced, and that constitutes a massive capital profit.

Unless the skills, resources, and productivity of the older work force are maintained in the economy, we will have a serious problem with inflation and unemployment. Whenever the money supply is increased without a corresponding growth of goods and services, there is an increase in inflation. At the same time as younger and less experienced employees are given professional opportunities, it is crucial that older and more experienced employees be maintained in the work force in order for the productivity in the economy to correspond to the money supply growth.

Both educators and employers have already recognized that their students and their employees are mutually enriched by the expanded instructional resources brought together by cooperating. Some of the most effective collaborative education projects are those that serve adults; however, adults are not usually enrolled as full-time students, and the part-time participation phenomenon presents certain design difficulties. One of these is the academic credit issue. Many of the collaborative education and work projects are challenging the academic credit barriers which operate within higher education. Some of the original ACE projects and New York State Board of Regents projects in evaluating and accrediting noncollegiate sponsored instruction have been important in chipping away at these earlier barriers.

One of the most significant conditions to establish effective collaboration is a very high level of support at the top of both organizations. The president of the institution and the ranking officer of the corporation must be fully dedicated to the success of a collaborative program or it is doomed to fail. Support staffs must be willing to make the counseling, registration, and teaching changes which are necessary. Operating relationships between the two partners must be agreed upon and formalized because institutional identity is at stake for both partners as they begin to blur the lines between their respective former roles.

Another practical issue is that of counseling. Earlier pilot programs recognized the need for on-site counseling, whether it be providing basic information, helping with important decisions about what to study, and continued support and tutorial services, particularly for specially recruited target groups. Another practical issue is that of preparing the faculty. In order to teach effectively in collaborative programs, faculty members must have training in dealing with approaches for adults.

Increasing the number and spectrum of collaborative arrangements depends upon a series of remaining issues. For program developers, the issues include studies of costs and benefits of collaborative programs and the effects of such programs upon the learners. Also, the planning, procedures, and expected outcomes of such work/education programs need further delineation. For employers, the issues remaining are: How do the employers select among competing institutional resources? How do they provide counseling to their employees? How do they deal with the barriers of employees who do not have readily accessible funds to pay tuition costs in a reimbursement program?

For the federal sector, the issues are much more complex. Their existing policies on indirect costs and financial aid directly discourage collaborative institutional relationships. Federal policy for determining indirect cost rates actually militate against the development of consortia. Because consortia are important in developing collaborative programs, the usually lower negotiated indirect cost rate is a federal policy that directly discourages institutions from applying for federal grants in order to develop education/work collaboration.

Federal policy on financial aid to less than halftime students deters both students and institutions from pursuing and offering joint degree programs. The part-time learner can rarely handle more than six hours each term. To consider enrolling in two institutions simultaneously becomes nearly impossible, therefore, for this would result in cutting off of any available financial aid.

For the states, an issue remaining is whether or not they should allow collaborative programs to emerge on a volunteer basis or whether they should get into the business of establishing regulatory policies. Some states, such as Illinois and Minnesota, do award state funds to encourage collaborative activity. AACJC, ASTD, and AVA will cosponsor an important national assembly in 1980 to address the questions of the roles of community colleges and employers in adult training for occupational and technical roles. ASTD includes nearly 20,000 human resource trainers and developers in the industrial and corporate arenas. We are meeting jointly with them to design better communication in the "field" as well as in our national offices and more appropriate and supportive ways to conduct cooperative education programs in the future.

Affirmation of Equity Goals

Although lifelong education is an idea and set of policies whose time has at last arrived, it is not a new idea. In fact, adult education and adult learning are concepts as old as education itself. In recent times, however, lifelong education has become a rallying point around which educators, politicians, and social reformers are grouping. However, the federal role should emphasize the development of equitable policies which assure that all groups have access to lifelong learning.

This means that we need new definitions of part-time and adult students in order to provide for student assistance. We need technical assistance programs to end age discrimination. We need to rewrite existing enabling legislation creating programs which offer educational and occupational information. We need to emphasize in such a system information which is both comprehensible and accessible to student consumers. There is also a need to create special training programs to develop a core of people who are trained personnel for lifelong learning. This would include teachers, counselors, brokers, and others.

Efforts are already underway to change the policies which describe the criteria for aid to independent students. There is also a specific need to undertake a cost-benefit research study to establish what the economic return and what the personal and social return of lifelong education is both to their students and to their community. Another specific need is to establish activities in several states in order to eliminate statutory barriers surrounding unemployment insurance which prevent people from continuing their education and training.

It will also be important to change the student financial aid program in order to allow fuller participation by adult part-time learners. A specific activity which community colleges could undertake is an initiative to convene all providers in a local area, for instance in a community learning opportunities council or in conjunction with a local educational information center, in order to gather the support necessary to address the financial aid needs of students and also to address the funding formulas at the state level. One outgrowth of this might be conducting the public hearings discussed earlier. At the leadership level it is important for college presidents, state commissioners, board chairpersons, and corporate executives to engage in a dialogue about the equity to be guaranteed to adult learners. This has to do specifically with economic development and cost-benefit in lifelong education.

As the quality of human resources is enriched, the quality of the democratic process is likewise improved. We need to make the arguments about improvement of citizen education and improvement of community development.

Conclusion

There are millions of Americans who have reaped the benefit of lifelong education in their personal lives. These benefits are reflected in the growth of our educational system in the last decade; the system has greatly diversified to meet the new needs for lifelong education. Adult students seeking out opportunities which are realistic and convenient have found themselves in learning situations that place them in schools, in colleges, in churches, in local and state libraries, in museums of every description, in large and small businesses, in organized labor unions, in the armed forces, and in other community action agencies. Each of these developed responsive educational services to fill existing needs not being met by the community college and university structure of our nation. People have pursued education in the arts and sciences, they have pursued education for better jobs and for new occupations, and there is currently a great increase in education for leisure. Adults are interested in learning—at more times and places, and in more new subjects—than ever before. One useful outgrowth of this expanded learning has been the patterns of cooperation which have developed among providers of learning services.

As is usually the case with social movements, it is now time for the policy framework to catch up. State and federal laws, state and federal administrative regulations, and boards of trustees guidelines in establishing institutions and cooperative patterns need to be revised. Funding formulas and other areas of financial support in order to sustain and encourage lifelong education need to be brought up to date. Also there are needs for a further research to develop the data to change attitudes about policies and procedures for offering lifelong education. People are of different ages, and substantially different ethnic make-up, than they were when our educational structure was established. Assessments of educational needs—asking the question about who the students are and what it is that they want to learn—are the next crucial steps in making the educational system responsive to citizens. We have already seen—by the very rich tapestry of existing lifelong learning opportunities—that where colleges are not "up to the challenge" they simply will be left out of the adult learning structure in the future.

This is a massive challenge. It will require activity at the local level, at the state level, at the city and county level, at the regional level, and at the federal level. It will also be critically important to involve the adult learners themselves in each of these activities because the nature of change is itself changing. Changes in adult learning and lifelong education are faster, more fundamental, more irreversible, more widespread, and more technologically complex than ever before. Serving lifelong learners means making them an integral part of the process rather than consumers of the product.

References

Gilder, J. (Ed.). *Policies for Lifelong Education: Report of the 1979 Assembly.* Washington, D.C.: American Association for Community and Junior Colleges, 1979. 128 pp. (ED 168 668—available in microfiche only)

"Lifelong Learning: Trustee Leadership in Local Linkages." Forum at AACJC Annual Convention, Chicago, May 1979.

Weathersby, J., and Jacobs, B. *Institutional Goals and Student Goals.* ERIC publication No. 2, 1977.

Jamison Gilder is director of the Policies for Lifelong Education
Project at the American Association of Community and
Junior Colleges.

Is your college up to redefining its roles in serving lifelong learners?
Six key indexes to institutional transformations are explored.

On Transforming a Traditional College

Barry Heermann

There are in this country a few community colleges, fewer than you can count on the fingers of one hand, that were designed from their inception as alternative and flexible programs for adult learners. The Community College of Vermont is one example. The kind of flexible time/space programs, so compatible with the life/career/learning patterns of adults, which these colleges celebrate, are not part of the postsecondary mainstream.

   Probably there will be only a few new colleges like these committed to flexible, alternative programming for adults. The whirlwind days of the 1960s, when for a period of time one new two year college was created every week of the year, will not be characteristic of the 1980s. The possibilities for radically new colleges, featuring new delivery services which recognize the prior learning of adult learners, integrating community resources with college resources, and providing individualized learning experiences external to the classroom is extremely remote.

   The best hope for adult learners is that existing colleges might creatively redefine and restructure their resources and delivery capabilities. Most adult learners (Tough, 1978) do not find our institutions comfortable places in which to learn, respectful of their uniqueness and autonomy. Community colleges as "islands of innovation"? Perhaps, but most adults are unimpressed: the 500 hours of learning endeavor they engage in yearly (on the average—see

Tough, 1978) is self-guided, independent, external study with only infrequent linkage to postsecondary educational institutions.

Those institutions which continue to serve adult learners in the 1980s with 1960s educational delivery will be of decreasing utility to their communities. The 1970s preoccupation with new programs of study must in the 1980s give way to new ways to learn—highly individualized, experiential, community-based learning that makes sense to adults and possesses an integrity superior to passive, abstract classroom exercises.

But institutional change is tricky business. The struggle will be to carefully conceive strategies which cause institutional transformation. I am fortunate enough to be with an urban college, with all of the traditional characteristics of most postsecondary institutions, that underwent such a transformation. At this institution some 150 traditional, teaching faculty persons participate in evaluating the prior learning of adult persons and negotiating individualized study experiences for 3,000–4,000 registrations annually. Achieving such a reorientation is not an exercise in black magic; it involves careful and thorough consideration of a half dozen fundamental considerations.

Test yourself. See if your institution has given adequate attention to the factors elaborated in the following pages:

- Lifelong learning institutional mission
- Administrative commitment to lifelong learning
- Organizational design for lifelong learners
- Redefinition of faculty roles and fiscal underpinnings
- Program development
- Institutional acceptance

Institutional mission. Check your mission statement. If commitment to serving lifelong learners with alternative, flexible, and experiential components is lacking, you have identified the first problem. Goals and objectives ought to flow out of institutional mission. If lifelong learners go unnoticed, then work hard at "consciousness raising" about the reality of the times, changing demographics, and adult learning (for instance, that most adults learn best independently, that they often bring college-equivalent learning from prior experience to their college enrollment, and so on).

Administrative Commitment. I hear it over and over again from faculty in my role as a consultant: "We understand the need to rethink and redesign our offerings for adults, but administration doesn't provide the resources (remuneration, release time, leadership) to make it possible." In some cases the blame is accurately placed; in others there is support, but faculty do not "own" their responsibility to move forward. One thing is clear: if there is not support from the top administrative officer through middle level program managers, then very little is going to get done. Structural and fiscal changes are strategic, and faculty in most institutions are powerless to affect their systems. Venture capital is an essential notion to instituting the kinds of changes necessary to begin meeting the needs of lifelong learners, and that kind of investment hinges on administrative action.

Organizational Design. In my experience organizational considerations are pivotal to the kind of reorientation and reallocation of resources that adult learners deserve. There are essentially three organizational patterns for presenting flexible and alternative lifelong learning programs: the free-standing organization; the traditional organization with adjunct service capability; and the traditional organization with integrated service capability.

I have alluded to the free-standing organizational arrangement wherein a college diverts all of its resources to nontraditional learning services. Empire State College at the four year level and Community College of Vermont at the two year level are examples. The improbability of more new institutions of this sort has already been noted.

A more common practice at the four year level (less so among two year colleges) is the creation of a unique organizational component as an adjunct to the existing departmental and divisional structures. The University of Alabama's New College, DePaul University's School for New Learning, or a number of University Without Walls programs housed in existing universities serve as models of this kind of organization.

Frequently these programs employ their own faculty, create their own curriculum, and award their own degree. This kind of organizational arrangement serves to circumvent traditional faculty resistances, allowing what is essentially a two track system. Traditional teaching faculty are not bothered with the new students or the new techniques, maintaining the purity of their classroom based lecture and testing modes, sidestepping the tension of new roles. The nontraditional component of the college has the flexibility of staffing persons committed to educational reform and skillful in individualized and experiential education for adults.

A third possibility is the integration of flexible lifelong learning throughout the institution. In this model traditional departments and teaching faculty take on roles as faculty evaluators of prior experiential learning, as faculty mentors of special individualized learning projects, or as core faculty who serve in an advocacy role, assisting lifelong learners in degree planning and learning contract development. Nontraditional educational delivery becomes the providence of all departments avoiding sensitive "turf" issues. Sinclair Community College is one example of such an organizational movement.

While the free-standing and adjunct models have compelling advantages, it is my position that the integrated model offers the greatest prospect for institutionalizing lifelong learner services, for serving significant numbers of lifelong learners, and for maintaining quality assurance (the same faculty who ensure standards for conventional instruction are responsible for quality control of unconventional, nonclassroom learning).

Redefinition of Faculty Roles and Fiscal Underpinnings. Regardless of organizational arrangement there is an optimum relationship of central-ized and decentralized services. In the integrated model, traditional teaching faculty have full authority for evaluating learning and awarding credits and grades. This authority is appropriately decentralized to departmental levels. However, there is considerable merit in a centralized office which recruits stu-dents, develops instructional materials, conducts inservice training, oversees the logistics and paperwork (a task of considerable dimension in programs serving large numbers of adults engaged in individualized study), accounts for reimbursement, and links students and faculty persons together in considera-tion of prior learning portfolios, learning contracts, and other independent activities.

The distinction between centralization and decentralization of author-ity serves also to differentiate line and staff relationships. In the integrated model, line authority, or the authority to control the delivery of instruction, is in the hands of existing departments and faculty. Staff authority is entrusted in the central office, whose sole function is to support, advise, and serve deans, departmental heads, and on-line faculty. This office acts as a catalyst and energizer for the college's nontraditional offerings, but the academic consider-ations are always a teaching faculty responsibility.

Serving lifelong learners with individualized, experiential, and flexible learning options necessitates the institution's rethinking of faculty roles. Fac-ulty need to be unshackled from traditional position definitions to accomplish the kind of personalized services suggested in this edition. Two primary roles for serving adult learners need to be provided: evaluator roles to ascertain the extent and college equivalency of prior experiential learning, and mentor roles to support and guide the student in the process of planning individualized learning experiences supportive of learning goals. There are other roles: core faculty roles and portfolio development faculty roles (wherein faculty provide advocacy and assistance in the development of learning contracts or portfolios of prior learning).

All this individualization can be cost effective. Not only are there sig-nificantly larger numbers of adults who respond to opportunities to move at their own pace, exercising a major role in the design of their learning exper-iences, but the cost revenue relationships can be adjusted in such a way as to underwrite all of the costs incurred. (For example, colleges with twenty-to-one FTE ratios for traditional three-credit courses, frequently accept ratios of twelve- or fifteen-to-one for seminars or advanced courses. Accordingly, inde-pendent student faculty arrangements which reimburse faculty at one-fifth of a pay hour per student in a three-credit enrollment maintain the same cost reve-nue relationships as a seminar).

Role redefinition and revisions in compensation go hand in hand. Too often the latter does not accompany the former, limiting faculty participation of any significant degree. The willingness to take on new faculty roles is much more a function of perceived social and ego threats than economic factors, in my experience. (The entire consideration of achieving institutional acceptance will be briefly considered below.)

Program Development Variables. Providing flexible, experiential programs for adult learners requires curriculum and institutional development. These alternatives require a fair amount of sophistication to put in place, necessitating an astute program developer, familiar with adult learning theory and experiential education. This expertise is typically not available in most institutions.

Fortunately there is a way that an ambitious faculty person or administrator committed to serving lifelong learners can develop the necessary competence. The Council for the Advancement of Experiential Learning represents the greatest technical capability in the arena of lifelong learning. Their extensive resources, including circuit-riding consultants and the best literature on lifelong and experiential learning, is readily available to its institutional members. Affiliation with CAEL is a desirable first step in the development of new options for adults. There is within CAEL a two year college emphasis, called the Community College Network.

This technical competence can be nurtured through visitation to exemplary programs (see the ERIC Topical Paper, *Experiential Learning in Community College*), and there are numerous skillful consultants who assist two year colleges in developing these skills (CAEL is an excellent referral for such persons).

The Fund for Improvement of Postsecondary Education and Title I, administered through state higher education commissions, encourage flexible time/space programs for lifelong learners. Institutions may apply for federal assistance or for endowment support in order to underwrite development as well as initial implementation.

Curriculum and instructional development should focus on: careful descriptions of educational processes; faculty and student guides and handbooks; standards for valid and reliable assessment; definitions for college equivalent learning in participating curricular areas; quality assurance safeguards; and materials to undergird the process (such as portfolio models for articulating and documenting prior learning or learning contracts for clarifying outcomes, experiences, and evaluation of sponsored nonclassroom learning exercises). This developmental phase is crucial and, without question, the literature published by CAEL represents the best available on lifelong education.

Achieving Institutional Acceptance. All the preceding is to no avail without a thorough consideration of "change strategy." It should be an overriding concern. Too many institutions have developed elaborate and thoughtfully conceived programs for assessing experiential learning of lifelong learners only to find crippling faculty resistance.

The problem? In my experience some program planners are inclined to impose their designs, concentrating staff development efforts on knowledge and skill development of faculty without concern for attitudes. Faculty have very deep-seated notions about the circumstances and locations of learning. In most institutions, to simply decree new roles is to ensure resentment and resistance. Attitudes of faculty must first be modulated. They need to be acquainted with exemplary programs, adult learning patterns, and rationale for nonclassroom and alternative learning options for adults.

The most successful staff development moves from attitudes to knowledge and skill development. The targets of change strategy should include the key constituencies of the college: faculty, students, administrators, trustees, advisory committees, education policy committees, state controlling boards, and community groups and officials. The approaches to change should vary with each group. Advisory committees formed for the purpose are exceedingly supportive of experiential programs. Many of their members were experientially trained and value work experience as a means to developing competence. Don't forget state controlling boards, to whom new credit mechanisms without classroom linkages are quite new, and for whom the compelling educational benefits of such programs need to be carefully documented.

A pivotal consideration to the whole notion of achieving institutional acceptance is the person selected as "change agent." The person must be interpersonally effective and sensitive to the educational issues involved. Ideally this person would be currently on the staff, enjoying the trust and acceptance of a breadth of faculty and administrative staff. An evangelistic commitment to educational reform, coupled with a high energy level, are aspects of the profile. Management and fiscal skills are invaluable in implementation phases. A rare person? Yes, but if such a program is to be successfully launched, it will require the appointment of a person skillful in these regards.

Participation of a cross section of staff is essential. A nonparticipating approach is potentially destructive to the full acceptance of the alternatives alluded to in these pages. An excellent approach is the appointment of a task group to investigate and study institutional options. Again, my experience would suggest the change agent or program manager will need to give primary initiative to evolving policy and developing inservice materials and program resources for the committee's consideration.

In conclusion, developing institutional competence in serving lifelong learners is best learned experientially. Faculty will experience the reward of overseeing experiential projects or assessing adults experientially trained, administrators will come to appreciate its contribution to adult learning and the new student clientele it will reach, and the community will be enriched by a college purveying new and viable services to its constituents.

References

Heermann, B. *Experiential Learning in the Community College.* Los Angeles, Calif.: ERIC Clearinghouse for Junior Colleges, 1977. 84 pp. (ED 140 909)

Tough, A. "Major Learning Efforts: Recent Research and Future Directions." In K. P. Cross and others (Eds.), *The Adult Learner: Current Issues in Higher Education, 1978.* Washington, D.C.: American Association for Higher Education, 1978.

Barry Heermann has served as a dean and director for Experience Based Education at Sinclair Community College, which includes College Without Walls, Credit for Lifelong Learning, and Field Education programs. He is coordinator of the Council for the Advancement of Experiential Learning's "Community College Network," and is a CAEL Regional Manager for the East Central States.

This chapter presents a review of documents in the ERIC system which describe programs making lifelong learning opportunities available to the public.

Increasing Opportunities for Lifelong Learning

Jack Friedlander

Community colleges attempt to extend their educational programs to a maximum number of people. However, as Knoell notes, even "the most accessible, most comprehensive community colleges still fall short of enrolling a student body which is fully representative of the communities being served" (1973, p. 107). Adults sometimes avoid participating because of job and family responsibilities, financial barriers, physical handicaps, inadequate transportation, unwillingness to attend classes on a college campus due to personal, psychological, or educational reasons, and lack of information about educational learning opportunities. New programs designed to make lifelong learning opportunities easily accessible to all citizens are promoted and introduced by federal agencies, state consortiums, and individual community colleges. Documents available in the ERIC system which describe some of the most innovative of these programs are cited in this final chapter.

Policies Affecting Lifelong Learning

An informative series of papers concerned with the role of community colleges in implementing federal legislation (The Education Amendments of 1976) related to lifelong learning can be found in a report edited by Furlong and others (1977). These papers, based on a national conference attended by representatives of many local, state, and federal agencies, are concerned with provisions in the legislation pertaining to lifelong learning and state planning, community colleges and postsecondary education planning, educational information centers, regional consortiums, education brokering, and noninstitutionalized postsecondary education delivery systems.

Papers presented at a conference on policies for lifelong education, sponsored by the American Association of Community and Junior Colleges, are available in a monograph edited by Gilder (1979). The reports focus on a wide range of legislative policies, institutional practices, and college programs that affect community colleges' ability to make their educational services readily accessible to all segments of the population. A comprehensive list of recommendations on policies which colleges should follow in providing lifelong education to all members of the community is provided.

The progress and projects of various countries in adapting higher education to lifelong learning are described by Gareth (1977). Other topics discussed in this book sponsored by the United Nations Educational, Scientific, and Cultural Organization (UNESCO) are counseling, the psychology of adult learning, methods of teaching, staff development, finance and the source of funds, and planning and organization.

Educational Information Centers

The purpose of educational information centers is to provide educational information, educational and careers planning, and referral services for all persons who might benefit from postsecondary education. These centers, most often funded by a combination of federal and foundation grant money plus user fees, are designed to link adult learners (including those who formerly would have never considered postsecondary education) with the wide diversity of educational resources available in their community. These include educational programs sponsored by public or private colleges and universities, proprietary schools, school district-sponsored programs, community college programs, employer or labor union-sponsored programs, community and church-sponsored programs as well as federal, state, and local government agency offerings (Furlong and others, 1977).

An excellent description of educational brokerages can be found in a monograph prepared by Heffernan and others (1976). The following topics are covered: definition and introduction to educational brokerages, services, clients, staff, organization structure, relationship with other institutions, reaching-out strategies, sources of funding, and evaluation of services. A directory of eighteen brokering programs is provided.

The regional approach to postsecondary education in Minnesota is described in a publication by the Minnesota Higher Education Coordinating Board (*Regional Center Approach* . . . , 1977). The primary goal of the center is to meet efficiently and effectively through increased cooperation among area

institutions the educational needs of individuals living in the region. Generally, the students are adults for whom access to college is difficult because of
job and family responsibilities. The centers do not offer degrees, but through
the use of joint schedules, joint advertising services, and other means, students
may select courses and earn degrees from participating institutions that bring
their resources (faculty, courses, and so on) to the project area. A description
of how one of the Minnesota regional postsecondary education centers is
attempting to bring potential students and potential cooperating institutions
together is discussed by Wakefield (1977).

Cooperative Arrangements with Business

In an effort to better serve the learning and manpower needs of employees and employers, many community colleges have established cooperative
educational programs with local businesses, industries, labor unions, and government agencies. An annotated bibliography is available consisting of twen-
ty-eight documents in the ERIC system which pertain to cooperative efforts
between community colleges and business, industry, labor unions, and government (*An Annotated Bibliography . . . ,* 1979). Included in this bibliography
are papers providing an overview of community college relationships and programs developed with local institutions, reporting results of manpower and
needs assessment studies, describing various cooperative education programs,
and discussing the role representatives from business, industry, and labor can
play in regard to community college advisory committees.

Hutton (1977) has noted that the United Automobile, Aerospace, and
Agricultural Implement Workers of America (UAW), as well as other unions,
have negotiated tuition and educational benefits of up to 900 dollars a year per
member. Yet only approximately two percent of the UAW members are availing themselves of these opportunities. Community colleges need to provide
workers with educational programs and services that are relevant and easily
accessible. In order to achieve this objective, Hutton recommends that colleges appoint full-time coordinators to work with unions to develop programs;
include representatives from labor on advisory committees; provide educational and career counseling to union members; and offer courses in union halls
and other locations near the workers' home and place of employment.

Johnson County Community College conducted a needs assessment to
identify course areas in which employers would like their employees to have
instruction (*Educational Needs of Johnson County Businesses,* 1978). About half of
the company representatives interviewed felt their employees preferred classes
which provided credit or certificate of completion, were held evenings and
weekends, met four hours or less per week, and could be completed in six
months or less with most workers preferring less than three months. About
one third of the representatives noted that there was adequate space at their
company to hold classes.

Flexible Scheduling

The assumption that education is the learner's major activity and that it takes place on weekdays between the hours of 9 A.M. and 5 P.M. creates scheduling problems for large numbers of potential part-time learners who wish to combine educational activities with other adult responsibilities. To eliminate this barrier to participation in formal learning activities a number of colleges are offering courses during nonbusiness hours (before 8 A.M., weekends, evenings) to enable adults to attend classes which, otherwise, they would be unable to attend due to time constraints. A number of methods of delivering instruction to students participating in learning activities during nontraditional times and/or in off-campus locations are described by Hutchins (1977).

The Universities Studies and Weekend College Program at Wayne State University (Michigan) is described by Feinstein and Angelo (1977). The program has close links with several institutions in the community. Classes are held in union halls, public libraries, in the meeting places of community organizations, corporation and government facilities, prisons, and on campus. The programs' innovative delivery system, curricular content, organizational structure, instructional methods, recruitment techniques, and student services can each be viewed as a valuable model for those attempting to plan or improve their colleges' lifelong learning programs.

The advantages of using individualized, self-paced instruction in conjunction with an open-entry-open-exit calendar at small, rural colleges are outlined by Gausman (1978). The investigator found that such a system increases enrollment by coordinating the entry and exit from college with the harvest season; and it increases enrollment by providing more flexible scheduling to fit part-time as well as full-time employees' time and location needs.

Open College, a division of Miami-Dade Community College, offers opportunities for academic work to persons finding it difficult to attend campus classes or feeling they can pursue academic work without class meetings. Credit courses are presented through a multimedia system of television, radio, and audiovisual cassettes in conjunction with printed materials and a computer-based feedback system for individualized instruction. Descriptions of the courses offered, enrollments, and student success (retention, grades) are reported by Anandam (1977).

Several authors in this volume and elsewhere (Hutchins, 1977; Lucas, 1975; Thompson, 1977) have pointed out that important college support services such as instructional skills laboratories, counseling, financial and advisement, job placement services, and student activities available on campus during daytime hours are frequently not extended to students participating in courses at nontraditional times or in off-campus locations. To illustrate, Thompson (1977) found that a large number of students enrolled in the evening classes of a community college desired more information about financial aid, access to the college's counseling and placement services, meetings with an assigned advisor, and availability of campus programs and activities at times appropriate to evening students.

Informing the Public

The educational opportunities provided by a college are of potential value only to those who know about them and who have accurate perceptions on how the programs are relevant to their educational needs. While this assertion seems apparent, lack of information continues to be a major barrier preventing many adults from participating. Results of in-depth interviews of community leaders and citizens in seven diverse California communities led Peterson and others (1975) to conclude that the most immediate problem in adjusting educational resources to interests does not appear to be the creation of new programs but rather the need for better publicity, information, and distribution of existing programs. Excerpts from a comprehensive guide on courses available in the community designed by the Santa Cruz Office of Education are provided both as an illustration of the resources available to adults in that county and also as a model of what other communities could do to meet citizens' need for information.

Hardig (1976) studied the ways in which adult students and nonparticipants in six Illinois public community college districts learned of the course offerings at their college. The highest percentage of the individuals surveyed indicated that they first learned of the course offerings through word of mouth (teacher or counselor at the college, friend or neighbor, coworker). This was followed by course schedules, college catalogues, flyers concerning the course, newspaper advertisement, student requests for information, and newspaper stories. Suggestions obtained from adult students, nonparticipants, and business and industry representatives on how the college could better inform them or their employees of the course offerings at the college are provided.

The Virginia Region Three Adult Education Coordinating Committee instituted a cooperative project designed to inform area residents of available adult education opportunities and to establish a central information contact point (Eyler, 1977). A list of adult education courses and services offered by participating institutions was created, newspaper and radio advertisements were developed, and a central information service center was established. A poll of those enrolled in adult education courses revealed that one fourth of the students were aware of the advertising or had called the adult education telephone number. The advertising scripts, response forms, and a financial statement of the project are presented in this report.

Slettehaugh (1978) obtained questionnaire and interview data from individuals in twelve communities which had developed comprehensive directories of adult learning opportunities available to the public. Information was acquired on the directories' content, purposes, funding source, costs, and methods of publicity and distribution. The investigator concluded that the most useful directories dealt with a limited geographic area, and that agency and volunteer cooperation made it possible to develop and distribute directories with little funding. Useful recommendations concerning the development of directories of adult learning opportunities are provided.

Some of the most creative methods currently being employed by community colleges to inform citizens of institutional offerings are described in the twenty-three papers cited in Rinnander's (1977) ERIC Review, "Recruiting Adult Students." Descriptions of approaches community colleges are using to attract such groups as senior citizens, retirees, women, members of ethnic minorities and ghetto youth groups traditionally underrepresented in postsecondary education are especially valuable.

Experiential Learning

The conventional notion that certifiable learning requires physical presence in the classroom restricts access to higher education for literally thousands of people who wish to earn an academic degree or certificate but who are unable or unwilling to do so through attending traditional campus-based courses (Cross and Jones, 1972). One approach many colleges are taking to reduce this barrier to participation in their program is to award credit for experiential learning. Experiential education is often discussed under the headings of prior learning and sponsored learning.

Prior learning includes any type of creditable learning — through work, travel, volunteer service, or self-directed accomplishments — that a student may have acquired independent of an educational institution and, typically, prior to matriculation (Heermann, 1977). Granting credit for prior learning is based on the premise that individuals should receive recognition for what they have learned without regard for where they acquired that knowledge.

Sponsored learning refers to institutionally sponsored programs that enable students to satisfy course and degree requirements in off-campus settings via work programs, internships, practicums, service activities, and community projects. Advocates of experiential learning contend that it is a ". . . particularly appropriate vehicle for adult learners who are seeking further education for personal and career development, since it recognizes that adults' work and volunteer experiences may form the basis for their academic program" (Shulman, 1978, p. 2). Excellent treatments of experiential education — the rationale, history, current programs, and major issues surrounding its implementation — can be found in Duley and Gordon (1977), Heermann(1977), Kray (1977), Shulman (1978), Stevens (1977), and Stutz and Knapp (1977). Results of a survey comparing the practices and policies of community colleges in the six regional accrediting associations concerning the awarding of credit for CLEP exams, work experience, inservice professional training, military experience, travel, and courses taken in non-accredited institutions are reported in Young and Healy (1975).

Heermann (1977) points to the need for two-year colleges to incorporate experiential learning into their educational programs. Essential components required for a successful experiential learning program are discussed. The College Without Walls at Sinclair Community College (Ohio) is described in this monograph to illustrate the operation of a comprehensive experiential learning program.

Stevens (1977) found that a course designed to prepare the student for assessment of prior learning was the best way for Blackhawk College (Illinois) to provide assistance to the student in developing a portfolio for evaluation. The author recommended that the college implement an assessment preparation course. Included in this report are results of a survey of institutions offering an assessment preparation course for students attempting to receive college credit for their prior learning experiences. Reports pertaining to the experiential learning programs found in California's Community Colleges (*Another Time, Another Place . . .*, 1976), Illinois' William Rainey Harper College (Christensen, 1975), Deleware County Community College (Pennsylvania) and Minnesota's Lakewood Community College (Kray, 1977) are available in the ERIC system.

Referencs

These ERIC documents, unless otherwise indicated, are available on microfiche (MF) or in paper copy (PC) from the ERIC Document Reproduction Service (EDRS), Computer Microfilm International Corporation, P.O. Box 190, Arlington, Virginia 22210. The MF price for documents under 480 pages is $0.83. Prices for PC are as follows: 1–25 pages, $1.82; 26–50, $3.32; 51–75, $4.82; 76–100, $6.32. For materials having more than 100 pages, add $1.50 for each 25–page increment (or fraction thereof). Postage must be added to all orders.

Abstracts of these and other documents in the Junior College Collection are available upon request from the ERIC Clearinghouse for Junior Colleges, Room 96, Powell Library, University of California, Los Angeles, California 90024. Bracketed publication dates are approximate.

Anandam, K. *Annual Report for Open College, 1976–77*. Miami, Fla.: Miami-Dade Community College, 1977. 100 pp. (ED 156 272 — Available in microfiche only)

An Annotated Bibliography of ERIC Documents on Cooperative Efforts Between Community Colleges and Business, Industry, and Government. Los Angeles: ERIC Clearinghouse for Junior Colleges, 1979.

Another Time, Another Place . . . Proceedings of the Symposium on Credit for Prior and Experiential Learning (San Francisco, California, November 5, 1976. Sacramento: California State Postsecondary Education Commission, 1976. 74 pp. (ED 146 413)

Christensen, F. A. *Guidelines and Procedures for the Assessment of Experiential Learning and the Selection of Training of Field Experts. (CAEL Institutional Report No. 5. William Rainey Harper College*. Princeton, N.J.: Cooperative Assessment of Experiential Learning Project, 1975. 67 pp. (ED 148 855 — Available in microfiche only)

Cross, K. P., and Jones, J. Q. "Problems of Access." In S. B. Gould and K. P. Cross (Eds.), *Explorations in Non-Traditional Study.* San Francisco: Jossey-Bass, 1972.

Duley, J., and Gordon, S. *College-Sponsored Experiential Learning—A CAEL Handbook.* Columbia, Md.: Cooperative Assessment of Experiential Learning, 1977. 73 pp. (ED 148 481—Available in microfiche only)

Educational Needs of Johnson County Businesses. Overland Park, Kans.: Johnson County Community College, 1978. 28 pp. (ED 165 865)

Eyler, D. R. *A Telephone Based Regional Adult Education Information Service.* Weyers Cave: Virginia Region 3 Adult Education Coordinating Committee, 1977. 40 pp. (ED 136 886)

Feinstein, O., and Angelo, F. *To Educate the People. An Experimental Model for Urban Higher Education for the Working Adult.* Detroit, Mich.: Wayne State University, 1977. 154 pp. (ED 146 880)

Furlong, T. (Ed.), and others. *State Planning for Lifelong Learning: Improving Access for Adult Citizens.* Report of a national invitational conference, Orlando, Fla., February 20–22, 1977. 202 pp. (ED 163 845)

Gareth, W. *Towards Lifelong Education: A New Role for Higher Education Institutions. The Development of Higher Education Series.* Paris, France: United Nations Educational, Scientific, and Cultural Organization, 1977.

Gausman, C. H. *Curriculum Comprehensiveness in the Small/Rural Community College: Strategies for Getting More Out of Limited Resources.* Paper presented at First National Conference on Small/Rural Colleges, Blacksburg, Virginia, August 1978. 8 pp. (ED 167 223)

Gilder, J. (Ed.). *Policies for Lifelong Education: Report of the 1979 Assembly.* Washington, D.C.: American Association of Community and Junior Colleges, 1979. 128 pp. (ED 168 668—Available in microfiche only)

Hardig, R. J. *Relative Effectiveness of Dissemination Practices Used by Illinois Public Community Colleges in Adult and Continuing Education.* Unpublished paper, 1976. 165 pp. (ED 143 378)

Heermann, B. *Experiential Learning in the Community College. Topical Paper No. 63.* Los Angeles: ERIC Clearinghouse for Junior Colleges, 1977. 84 pp. (ED 140 909)

Heffernan, J. M., and others. *Educational Brokering: A New Service for Adult Learners.* Syracuse, N.Y.: National Center for Educational Brokering, 1976. 93 pp. (ED 136 833—Available in microfiche only)

Hutchins, E. C. *The Learning Needs of Adults in Hill County, Texas.* Hillsboro, Tex.: Hill Junior College, 1977. 60 pp. (ED 145 882)

Hutton, C. M. *The UAW and Education: A Collection of Statements by Carroll M. Hutton.* Detroit, Mich.: International Union, United Automobile, Aerospace, and Agricultural Implement Workers of America, 1977. 72 pp. (ED 164 016)

Knoell, D. M. (Ed.). "Those Not in College." In D. M. Knoell (Ed.), *New Directions for Community Colleges: Understanding Diverse Students,* no. 3. San Francisco: Jossey-Bass, 1973.

Kray, E. J. *Experiential Learning Assessment—A Sourcebook for Postsecondary Institutions.* Vols. 2 and 3. Unpublished paper, 1977. 395 pp. (ED 148 435)

Lucas, J. A. *Evaluation of Weekend and Early Morning Classes. Research Report Series, Vol. 7, No. 7.* Palatine, Ill.: William Rainey Harper College, 1975. 21 pp. (ED 118 189)

Peterson, R. E., and others. *Postsecondary Alternatives: Meeting California's Educational Needs. A Feasibility Study. First Technical Report, Part Two: Community Needs for Post secondary Alternatives.* Sacramento: California State Legislature, 1975. 228 pp. (ED 153 510)

Regional Center Approach Serves Residents Effectively. MHECB Report, 1977, *3* (6). St. Paul: Minnesota Higher Education Coordinating Board, 1977. 17 pp. (ED 150 905)

Rinnander, E. "Recruiting Adult Students." *Community College Review,* 1977, *5* (1), 55–60.

Shulman, C. H. *Implementing Experiential Learning for Adult Students. ERIC/Higher Education Research Currents.* Washington, D.C.: ERIC Clearinghouse on Higher Education, 1978. 5 pp. (ED 154 658)

Slettehaugh, S. A. *A Study of Comprehensive Adult Education Directories.* Unpublished paper, 1978. 92 pp. (ED 159 368)

Stevens, M. A. *Developing Learning Objectives for a Model Course to Prepare Adults for the Assessment of Prior, Non-Sponsored Learning by Portfolio Evaluation.* Unpublished paper, 1977. 48 pp. (ED 140 887)

Stutz, J. P., and Knapp, J. (Eds.). *Experiential Learning: An Annotated Literature Guide. (CAEL Project Report.)* Princeton, N.J.: Cooperative Assessment of Experiential Learning Project, 1977. 157 pp. (ED 148 859—Available in microfiche only)

Thompson, J. R. *An Evaluation of the Evening Programs at Everett Community College.* Unpublished paper, 1977. 85 pp. (ED 145 899)

Wakefield, W. "The Rochester Consortium." In T. Furlong (Ed.), *State Planning for Lifelong Learning: Improving Access for All Citizens.* Report of a national invitational conference, Orlando, Fla., February 20-22, 1977.

Young, J., and Healy, T. *Survey of Practices of Community Colleges in Granting Credit for Non-Traditional Learning Experiences.* Douglas, Ariz.: Cochise College, 1975. 43 pp. (ED 156 289)

Jack Friedlander is staff research associate at the ERIC Clearinghouse for Junior Colleges at UCLA in Los Angeles.

Index

New Directions Quarterly Sourcebooks

New Directions for Community Colleges is one of several distinct series of quarterly sourcebooks published by Jossey-Bass. The sourcebooks in each series are designed to serve both as *convenient compendiums* of the latest knowledge and practical experience on their topics and as *long-life reference tools.*

One-year, four-sourcebook subscriptions for each series cost $18 for individuals (when paid by personal check) and $30 for institutions, libraries, and agencies. Single copies of earlier sourcebooks are available at $6.95 each *prepaid* (or $7.95 each when *billed*).

A complete listing is given below of current and past sourcebooks in the *New Directions for Community Colleges* series. The titles and editors-in-chief of the other series are also listed. To subscribe, or to receive further information, write: New Directions Subscriptions, Jossey-Bass Inc., Publishers, 433 California Street, San Francisco, California 94104.

New Directions for Child Development
William Damon, Editor-in-Chief

New Directions for Continuing Education
Alan B. Knox, Editor-in-Chief

New Directions for Exceptional Children
James G. Gallagher, Editor-in-Chief

New Directions for Experiential Learning
Morris T. Keeton and Pamela J. Tate, Editors-in-Chief

New Directions for Higher Education
JB Lon Hefferlin, Editor-in-Chief

New Directions for Institutional Advancement
A. Westley Rowland, Editor-in-Chief

New Directions for Institutional Research
Marvin W. Peterson, Editor-in-Chief

New Directions for Learning Centers
Kurt V. Lauridsen, Editor-in-Chief

New Directions for Mental Health Services
H. Richard Lamb, Editor-in-Chief

New Directions for Methodology of Social and Behavioral Science
Donald W. Fiske, Editor-in-Chief

New Directions for Program Evaluation
Scarvia B. Anderson, Editor-in-Chief

New Directions for Student Services
Ursula Delworth and Gary R. Hanson, Editors-in-Chief

New Directions for Teaching and Learning
Kenneth E. Eble and John Noonan, Editors-in-Chief

New Directions for Testing and Measurement
William B. Schrader, Editor-in-Chief